In the Kitchen
THE COSTCO WAY ™

Apricot Martini can be found on page 183.

In the Kitchen
THE COSTCO WAY™

Fantastic recipes using Costco products

Tim Talevich
Editorial Director

With a foreword by
Sandra Lee

Issaquah, Washington

Senior Vice President E-commerce and Publishing:	Ginnie Roeglin
Publisher:	David W. Fuller
Editorial Director:	Tim Talevich
Art Director:	Doris Winters
Associate Art Director:	Lory Williams
Associate Editor:	Judy Gouldthorpe
Graphic Designer:	Dawna Tessier
Photographers:	Darren Emmens Devin Seferos Tom Clements
Food Stylists:	Amy Muzyka-McGuire Christine Jackson Tyler Rebman
Kitchen Manager:	Linda Carey
Studio Assistant:	Melissa Fraser
Business Manager:	Jane Klein-Shucklin
Advertising Manager:	Steve Trump
Advertising Assistants:	Melanie Woods Kathy Jabcuga
Advertising Copywriter:	Bill Urlevich
Production Manager:	Pam Sather
Assistant Production Manager:	Antolin Matsuda
Prepress Supervisor/ Color Specialist:	MaryAnne Robbers
Print Management:	James Letzel and William Ting, GSSI
Distribution:	Rossie Cruz Dorothy Strakele

All food photographs by Iridio Photography, Seattle, Washington, with the following exceptions:
George Lange © SLSH Enterprises, Inc., 7
Diamond Fruit Growers, 12 (top right)
Fowler Packing, 31 (top right)
General Mills, Pillsbury, 54 (top left)
Dulcinea Farms, 61 (top right)
NBC/Universal courtesy of Everett Collection, 89 (chef photo)
George Lange © SLSH Enterprises, Inc., 91 (chef photo)
Lori Balse, 95 (chef photo)
Sylvia Vidaurri, 99 (chef photo)
Christopher Hirsheimer, 109 (chef photo)
California Pear Advisory Board, 187 (top right)

FIRST EDITION

Printed by Daehan Printing Company, Seoul, South Korea

ISBN-13: 978-0-9819003-0-8
ISBN-10: 0-9819003-0-5
Library of Congress Control Number: 2008932919

41

135

33

195

Contents

To Our Valued Members

We are delighted to offer this gift—our seventh annual cookbook in our series of *Costco Way* cookbooks—to thank you for your business and loyal membership. This book has been made possible through the support of Costco's many food suppliers.

As in past years, we've asked our suppliers to develop recipes that showcase their products that we sell at Costco. We have also included recipes from many of our favorite celebrity chefs such as Sandra Lee, Martha Stewart, Ina Gartner and Paula Deen in the "Chef's Choice" section in the center of the book. These top chefs have worked their magic to develop recipes and tips using their favorite ingredients from Costco. Most of the recipes throughout the book have a short list of affordable, readily available ingredients and are quick and easy to prepare.

This year, you'll also find a new chapter, "Healthy Dishes." It's a perfect addition since many of us are trying to adopt a healthier lifestyle for ourselves and our families. You can also find healthy recipes in other parts of the book. For example, in our "Chef's Choice" chapter you'll find healthy and delicious recipes from Jessica Seinfeld, Myra Goodman and Ellie Krieger.

And yes, you can eat healthy and shop at Costco! We sell lots of fresh fruits and vegetables, lean meats, poultry, fish, nuts, olive oil, whole grain breads, whole wheat pasta and healthy snacks. You just can't eat the whole package in one sitting!

Of course, the secret to any great dish is using only top-quality ingredients. When you purchase your ingredients from Costco, you know that you are off to a great start. As Sandra Lee explains in her foreword on the next page, Costco does 70 percent of the work for you.

We hope you enjoy *In the Kitchen The Costco Way* and try out our recipes with your family and friends. You can also find our past years' cookbooks online at costco.com. Just type "Costco Cookbooks" in the search window on our home page.

Bon appétit from all of us at Costco!

Ginnie Roeglin,
Senior Vice President,
E-commerce and Publishing

Foreword

When I was a little girl, going to the grocery store was a big adventure. My Grandma Lorraine would settle my sister Cindy in the front of the cart, with me standing eagerly in back, and off we'd go, wheeling up and down the aisles in search of bargains we could whip up into fun family meals. Over the years, Grandma taught me which foods were pantry staples, which ones were comfort foods and which ones were pure luxury. I learned that eating well was possible on any budget, if you're thoughtful about the foods you buy and combine them creatively to make the ordinary extraordinary.

All those trips to the store are among my most cherished childhood memories, so it seems fitting that they evolved into the cornerstone of my unique Semi-Homemade® philosophy. Quality convenience products have always been the main ingredient in my 70/30 formula: Mix 70 percent ready-made products with 30 percent fresh foods, add a dash of your own creativity and take 100 percent of the credit for a meal that's fresh, fast and fabulous!

I love Costco because it does 70 percent of the work for you. Choice cuts of meats, fresh fruits and vegetables, frozen foods and pantry staples put all the ingredients of a nutritious meal right at your fingertips. It's a smart shopper's dream: gourmet chocolates just begging to be melted into a silky sauce; exotic-tasting syrups and spices ready to layer into a rich marinade or a savory rub; scrumptious store-bought desserts waiting for your personal embellishments. Best of all, it's right there in one place, everything you need to get a week's worth of meals on the table fast.

Think of cooking as a great adventure, filled with new things to try, new tastes to explore and new flavor combinations just waiting to be discovered. This cookbook, *In the Kitchen The Costco Way*, is the perfect place to start your explorations.

Eat well. Live well. Cheers to a happy, healthy life!

Costco member Sandra Lee's latest books are Semi-Homemade Money Saving Meals, Desserts 2 *and* Fast-Fix Family Favorites. *For more about Sandra, her recipes and her Semi-Homemade philosophy, see* www.SemiHomemade.com.

Sandra Lee

About This Book

In the Kitchen The Costco Way is the seventh in our series of cookbooks designed to showcase the exciting array of foods sold at Costco. It is being distributed free to our members on a first-come, first-served basis the weekend after Thanksgiving as a token of our appreciation for their membership.

In this year's book we are proud to present two special features. The nutritional content of recipes developed by healthy-eating expert Devin Alexander or submitted by our food suppliers is included with the recipes in the "Healthy Dishes" chapter beginning on page 10. For our "Kitchen Basics" section (page 85), we asked the legendary Martha Stewart to suggest her Top 10 kitchen tools, basic bakeware and essentials for stocking the pantry. She also developed three recipes for our "Chef's Choice" chapter (page 88) using our Kirkland Signature spices.

Our popular "Chef's Choice" chapter offers 30 pages of recipes developed by 10 of the country's most accomplished chefs. All of these chefs have achieved national renown with cookbooks of their own, television shows and/or exceptional restaurants. Thanks to all of them for helping to make this another exciting addition to *The Costco Way* cookbook series.

The rest of the book is arranged in a simple and direct manner with sections for breakfast, appetizers, salads and soups, side dishes, entrées, desserts and beverages. The index at the back of the book contains listings by recipe and food item. We also have included a "Supplier Listing" section with contact information for all of the participating food suppliers.

Every recipe in *In the Kitchen The Costco Way* has been identified with the supplier's name and logo. We want to thank each of these suppliers for their support of this book. (Please note that some branded products may not be sold in your part of the country. In such cases, you should substitute a similar product.)

I hope you will enjoy many wonderful meals using this book and that some of these dishes end up in your own collection of favorite recipes.

David W. Fuller,
Publisher

In the Kitchen
THE COSTCO WAY™

Healthy Dishes

Grape Pizza
Delano Farms

- 1 8-inch low-fat whole-wheat flour tortilla
- 3 tablespoons reduced-fat sour cream (2 grams of fat or less per 2-tablespoon serving)
- 2 teaspoons to 1 tablespoon brown sugar
- $1/2$ cup Delano Farms red seedless grapes, cut in half

Preheat oven to 400°F.

Place tortilla on a small nonstick baking sheet and bake for 3-4 minutes per side, or until it is completely crisp throughout. If air bubbles form during cooking, poke them with a fork, then use a spatula or oven mitt to carefully press the air out. Remove from the oven and let cool completely.

Transfer the tortilla to a cutting board and spread sour cream evenly over the top, leaving a small border around the edges. Sprinkle brown sugar to taste evenly over the sour cream. Top evenly with grapes, cut side down.

Cut into 4 wedges and serve immediately. Makes 1 serving.

Nutritional information: Each serving has 227 calories, 5 g protein, 46 g carbohydrates, 5 g fat, 2 g saturated fat, 15 mg cholesterol, 2 g fiber, 183 mg sodium.

Recipe courtesy of Devin Alexander.

Devin Alexander

There was a time not so long ago when the word "healthy" in association with food conjured images of wheatgrass and fake meat. Trust me, I know. I've been committed to cooking healthy and decadent foods for more than 20 years, and I've faced skeptic after skeptic. But I'm excited to say that we as a society are finally getting it.

We're coming to realize that fresher is actually better. We're seeking out flavorful, lower-calorie, lower-fat, lower-cholesterol, nutrient-rich foods that actually do taste as good as, if not better than, our old artery-clogging fallbacks.

I always say that 20 minutes in the kitchen can save you three hours on a treadmill. It's true. So often, restaurants are in such a huge hurry to get the next order out that they add oils or fats to even the simplest dishes, such as egg-white omelets, just so they don't stick to the pan. But at home, I can concentrate on the flavors I love and get rid of the fats I won't even miss.

Just by heading to my local Costco to pick up eggs, plenty of fresh veggies and even cheese, I can make a sinful yet guiltless omelet in my Circulon nonstick skillet (also available at Costco) with significantly less fat and fewer calories. I can also pick up the freshest of fruits and create an amazing fruit salad and serve it in martini glasses to make it even more special, all for a fraction of the cost (to both my health and my wallet) of eating out.

In this Healthy Dishes chapter, I hope you'll indulge in some of my favorites, such as Sweet-and-Sour Chicken Bowl, Pan-Fried Salmon with Mango Cucumber Salsa and even Peach Shortcake ... consequence-free!

Costco member Devin Alexander has maintained a 55-pound weight loss for more than 15 years and is committed to helping others find healthy comfort foods through her TV shows, best-selling cookbooks, foods and culinary products. She is the author of The Most Decadent Diet Ever!, The Biggest Loser Cookbook *and* The Biggest Loser Family Cookbook *(available at costco.com). For more from Devin, visit her Web site,* www.devinalexander.com.

Black and Blue Breakfast Smoothie Bowl
Alpine Fresh

1 1/2 cups Alpine Fresh* blueberries, bought fresh, then frozen

1 1/2 cups Alpine Fresh* blackberries, bought fresh, then frozen

1 medium banana

1/4 cup orange juice

8 ice cubes

2 teaspoons honey (optional)

1/2 cup low-fat granola without raisins

Take the fresh berries and freeze them shortly before making the recipe. Place the frozen berries, the banana, orange juice and ice in the jar of a blender. Blend on high speed until the mixture is almost smooth, with a texture between a slush and a sorbet.

Pour the mixture into a cereal bowl or glass. Stir in honey, if desired. Top with granola. Serve immediately. Makes 2 servings.

Nutritional information: Each serving has 284 calories, 5 g protein, 66 g carbohydrates, 2 g fat, trace saturated fat, 0 mg cholesterol, 12 g fiber, 70 mg sodium.

Recipe courtesy of Devin Alexander.
* Brands may vary by region; substitute a similar product.

Bibb Lettuce Salad with Gorgonzola and Fresh Pear Dressing
Diamond Fruit Growers

3 large ripe Diamond Fruit Growers* pears, divided

1/3 cup granulated sugar

1/2 teaspoon fresh tarragon or scant 1/4 teaspoon dried

1-2 tablespoons cider vinegar

1 1/2 tablespoons lemon juice

2-3 heads Bibb lettuce, rinsed and dried

4 ounces (1 cup) crumbled Gorgonzola or blue cheese

Peel, core and chop 1 pear. Place pear, 1/3 cup water, sugar and tarragon in a small saucepan. Simmer over medium heat until pear pieces are soft, about 5 minutes, depending on ripeness of pear. Do not let all the water evaporate. There should be about 7/8 cup pear and liquid. Remove from the heat and let cool.

Pour pear and liquid into a blender and blend until smooth. Add part of the vinegar and lemon juice. Taste and adjust sugar and acid to make a sweet-tart dressing, adding a little water if needed to thin. Refrigerate until cold.

Core and thinly slice remaining 2 pears.

For each serving, arrange 3-4 lettuce leaves on a salad plate. Top with 1/3 of a sliced pear and 2-3 tablespoons Gorgonzola. Drizzle with 2 tablespoons dressing. Serve immediately. Makes 6 servings.

Nutritional information: Each serving has 184 calories, 5 g protein, 32 g carbohydrates, 6 g fat, 4 g saturated fat, 18 mg cholesterol, 5 g fiber, 240 mg sodium.

Recipe by Heartline Café, Sedona, Arizona.
* Brands may vary by region; substitute a similar product.

French Bean Salad with Avocado and Mango
Los Angeles Salad Company

1 pound Los Angeles Salad Company trimmed French green beans

1 cup olive oil

1/2 cup lemon juice

Salt and pepper

1 1/4 cups diced fresh mango

1 1/4 cups diced fresh tomato

1 cup sliced green onions

1/2 tablespoon grated lemon peel

6 cups mixed baby greens

3 avocados

Cook beans in salted boiling water until al dente (about 3 minutes). Transfer into iced water, then drain. (This can be done ahead of time.)

In a large salad bowl, mix olive oil and lemon juice with salt and pepper to taste. Transfer two-thirds of this dressing to another bowl and mix in mango, tomato, green onions and lemon peel.

Add beans and mixed baby greens to the remaining dressing in the salad bowl and toss to coat. Mound the mixture in the center of 6 plates.

Cut avocados in half, remove the skin and cut each half into 5 wedges. Arrange the avocado wedges standing up against the French bean salad. Spoon the mango mixture over and around the salad. Makes 6 servings.

Nutritional information: Each serving has 552 calories, 5 g protein, 27 g carbohydrates, 51 g fat, 7 g saturated fat, 0 mg cholesterol, 12 g fiber, 38 mg sodium.

Recipe created by Jean-Pierre Bosc, Mimosa Restaurant, Los Angeles.

Layered Rice Pesto and Pepper Bake
Pacific International Rice Mill

Nonstick vegetable spray

3 cups cooked Homai Calrose* rice

1 3/4 cups shredded Parmesan cheese, divided

Salt and ground pepper

1/2 cup prepared basil pesto sauce, divided

4 ounces crumbled goat cheese, divided

10 ounces roasted red peppers, drained, patted dry and chopped, divided

Preheat oven to 400°F. Coat a 7-inch soufflé dish or springform pan with nonstick vegetable spray.

Combine rice, 1 1/2 cups Parmesan, and salt and pepper to taste in a medium bowl.

Place half of the rice mixture in the prepared dish; pat down well. Spread half of pesto evenly over rice and sprinkle with half of goat cheese. Layer half of red peppers over goat cheese. Repeat above layers. Sprinkle remaining 1/4 cup Parmesan over top.

Bake for 12-15 minutes, or until heated through. Cut into wedges to serve. Makes 6 servings.

Nutritional information: Each serving has 372 calories, 20 g protein, 24 g carbohydrates, 22 g fat, 11 g saturated fat, 42 mg cholesterol, 2 g fiber, 789 mg sodium.

Recipe supplied by USA Rice Federation.
* Brands may vary by region; substitute a similar product.

Apple Chicken Stir-Fry
Rainier Fruit Company

1 tablespoon plus 1 1/2 teaspoons vegetable oil, divided

1 pound cubed boneless, skinless chicken breast

1/2 cup vertically sliced onion

1 3/4 cups thinly sliced carrots

1 teaspoon dried basil, crushed

1 cup fresh or frozen Chinese pea pods

1 tablespoon water

1 medium Rainier* apple, cored and thinly sliced (Granny Smith, Golden, Pink Lady or Cameo)

2 cups cooked brown rice

Heat 1 tablespoon vegetable oil over medium-high heat in a nonstick skillet. Add chicken and stir-fry until lightly browned and cooked through. Remove from the skillet.

Heat remaining oil in the skillet. Add onions, carrots and basil; stir-fry until carrots are tender.

Stir in pea pods and water; stir-fry for 2 minutes.

Remove from the heat; stir in apple. Add chicken and stir to blend.

Serve hot over rice. Makes 4 servings.

Nutritional information: Each serving has 340 calories, 29 g protein, 37 g carbohydrates, 8 g fat, <1 g saturated fat, 60 mg cholesterol, 5 g fiber, 576 mg sodium.

Recipe courtesy of Produce for Better Health Foundation (PBH).
* Brands may vary by region; substitute a similar product.

Berry Spinach Salad
Curry & Company/Victoria Island Farms/ SunnyRidge Farm/Andrew & Williamson

8 cups spinach leaves, rinsed and spun dry

2 cups fresh blueberries

1 1/2 cups halved fresh strawberries

1 cup fresh blackberries

1/4 cup broken pecans, lightly toasted

DRESSING

1/2 cup halved strawberries

1/4 cup raspberry vinegar

Grated peel of 1 lemon

2 tablespoons freshly squeezed lemon juice

1 tablespoon light agave nectar or honey

2 teaspoons extra-virgin olive oil

Combine spinach, blueberries, strawberries and blackberries in a large bowl and toss gently.

To prepare the dressing, in a small bowl mash strawberries into a pulp. Add vinegar, lemon peel and juice, agave and olive oil. Stir well with a whisk.

Arrange the spinach and berry mixture on plates and drizzle with dressing. Sprinkle with toasted pecans. (Or drizzle the dressing over the spinach/berry mixture in the bowl, add pecans and then toss.) Makes 6 servings.

Nutritional information: Each serving has 140 calories, 3 g protein, 23 g carbohydrates, 6 g fat, <1 g saturated fat, 0 mg cholesterol, 5 g fiber, 170 mg sodium.

Recipe developed by Christine Jackson, food stylist.

Turkey Avocado Sprout Club Sandwiches
Milton's

12 slices Milton's* Multi-Grain Plus Bread

2 ripe avocados, peeled and sliced

1 package turkey deli meat (8-12 ounces)

1 bunch radishes, sliced

2 ounces alfalfa sprouts

8 ounces goat cheese, at room temperature

1/4 teaspoon salt (optional)

1/4 teaspoon pepper (optional)

Place bread slices under the broiler and toast until golden brown on both sides.

Place avocado slices on 8 pieces of toast. Top with turkey, radishes and sprouts. Crumble goat cheese over sprouts and season with salt and pepper.

Stack sandwiches together so that each sandwich has 2 layers of avocado, turkey, radishes, sprouts, and goat cheese and 3 slices of toast (1 on bottom, 1 in middle and 1 on top).

Cut in half and serve. Makes 4 servings.

Nutritional information: Each serving has 679 calories, 39 g protein, 55 g carbohydrates, 36 g fat, 15 g saturated fat, 73 mg cholesterol, 19 g fiber, 1,685 mg sodium.

Tip: Complement your lunch with Milton's* Gourmet Multi-Grain Crackers and your favorite dip or spread.

Brands may vary by region; substitute a similar product.

Hazelnut and Lemon French Green Beans
Alpine Fresh

1 pound Alpine Fresh* French green beans

1/2 teaspoon salt, plus more to taste

1 tablespoon and 1 teaspoon coarsely chopped hazelnuts, toasted

1 tablespoon grated lemon peel

1 tablespoon and 1 teaspoon lemon juice, preferably fresh-squeezed

1 teaspoon extra-virgin olive oil

Ground black pepper

Fill a large pot one-third full of water. Cover and set over high heat. When the water comes to a full boil, add beans and 1/2 teaspoon salt. Cook for 2-5 minutes, or until just tender. Drain in a colander.

Transfer the beans to a serving bowl. Add hazelnuts, lemon peel, lemon juice and olive oil. Season to taste with salt and pepper. Toss gently to mix. Serve immediately. Makes 4 servings.

Nutritional information: Each serving has 55 calories, 2 g protein, 8 g carbohydrates, 3 g fat (trace saturated), 0 mg cholesterol, 5 g fiber, 14 mg sodium.

Note: To toast hazelnuts, place in a dry nonstick skillet over high heat. Cook for 1-3 minutes, shaking every 15 seconds or so, until toasted. Watch closely, as they brown quickly.

Adapted from The Biggest Loser Cookbook *by Chef Devin Alexander and* The Biggest Loser *experts and cast with Karen Kaplan. Copyright (c) 2006 by Universal Studios Licensing LLLP,* The Biggest Loser™ *and NBC Studios, Inc., and Reveille LLC. By arrangement with Rodale, Inc.*

Brands may vary by region; substitute a similar product.

Cheesy Garden Veggie Quesadilla Triangles
Kellogg's

6 MorningStar Farms* Chipotle Black Bean Burger, Garden Veggie Patties *or* Gardenburger The Original, thawed

1 *each* red, yellow and green bell peppers, cut in 1/8-inch dice

1 cup shredded pepper jack cheese

1/2 cup shredded Cheddar cheese

1/2 cup shredded Monterey jack cheese

1 cup roasted tomato salsa

16 10-inch flour tortillas
Melted butter

CILANTRO LIME SOUR CREAM DIPPING SAUCE

4 ounces sour cream

1 1/2 tablespoons freshly squeezed lime juice

1 ounce fresh cilantro, minced

1/2 teaspoon each: ground cumin, chili powder, cayenne pepper, salt, black pepper

Preheat oven to 350°F.

Cut thawed burgers into 1/4-inch dice.

In a large mixing bowl, combine burger, peppers, cheese and salsa. Mix thoroughly and set aside.

Cut each tortilla into a 7-inch triangle.

Place 2 tablespoons of filling in the center of each triangle; fold each corner into the center, overlapping one another.

Brush quesadillas with melted butter and cook in a nonstick pan over medium heat until browned, about 1 minute per side. Place in the oven for 5 minutes, or until heated through.

To prepare the dipping sauce, combine all ingredients and mix well.
Makes 8 servings.

Nutritional information: Each serving has 770 calories, 28 g protein, 91 g carbohydrates, 32 g fat, 14 g saturated fat, 54 mg cholesterol, 8 g fiber, 1,850 mg sodium.

* Brands may vary by region; substitute a similar product.

Kellogg's®

Chicken Salad Dijon with Grapes and Apples
Delano Farms

1 pound boneless, skinless chicken breasts, visible fat removed

3 teaspoons extra-virgin olive oil, divided

Salt and pepper

3 tablespoons nonfat plain yogurt

3 tablespoons Dijon mustard

$1/3$ cup chopped celery

$1/3$ cup Delano Farms black seedless grapes, cut in half

$1/3$ cup chopped red apples

Lettuce leaves, for garnish (optional)

Preheat a grill to high heat.

Rub chicken on all sides with 1 teaspoon olive oil. Season to taste with salt and pepper. Grill on high for 3-5 minutes per side, or until the chicken is no longer pink inside. Let the chicken cool, then cut into bite-sized cubes.

Meanwhile, in a large glass or plastic mixing bowl, whisk together the remaining 2 teaspoons olive oil, yogurt and mustard. Add chicken, celery, grapes and apples. Gently toss the mixture well to combine. Season to taste with salt and pepper. Garnish with lettuce leaves, if desired. Makes 4 servings.

Nutritional information: Each $3/4$-cup serving has 174 calories, 27 g protein, 4 g carbohydrates, 5 g fat, <1 g saturated fat, 66 mg cholesterol, <1 g fiber, 234 mg sodium.

Recipe from The Biggest Loser Family Cookbook by Chef Devin Alexander and The Biggest Loser experts and cast with Melissa Roberson. Copyright (c) 2006 by Universal Studios Licensing LLLP, The Biggest Loser™ and NBC Studios, Inc., and Reveille LLC. By arrangement with Rodale, Inc.

Heart Healthy Stir-Fry
Andy Boy

2 tablespoons peanut or canola oil

1 cup of any of the following: beef strips, chicken chunks, shrimp or tofu chunks (mixing and matching is encouraged!)

2 cups chopped Andy Boy* romaine hearts

1 cup chopped Andy Boy* broccoli

1 cup chopped Andy Boy* broccoli rabe

$1/2$ cup chopped Andy Boy* cauliflower

$1/2$ cup chopped red bell pepper

$1/2$ cup chopped zucchini (optional)

2 tablespoons *each* soy sauce and rice vinegar, *or* 4 tablespoons hoisin sauce

3 garlic cloves, minced

1 teaspoon grated lemon peel

Cooked rice

Heat a wok (or heavy fry pan) over medium-high heat. Add oil. Add beef and stir-fry for 2 minutes (5-10 for shrimp, chicken and tofu), or until fully cooked.

Add all of the veggies. Toss vigorously, adding either soy sauce and rice vinegar or hoisin sauce. Continue tossing until the veggies soften to desired tenderness, about 2-3 minutes.

Turn off the heat and mix in garlic and lemon peel.

Serve over rice. Makes 4 servings.

Nutritional information: Each serving has 240 calories, 11 g protein, 15 g carbohydrates, 16 g fat, 3 g saturated fat, 24 mg cholesterol, 3 g fiber, 927 mg sodium.

Recipe courtesy of Chef Lou DeAngelis, Andy Boy Chef's Edge.
* Brands may vary by region; substitute a similar product.

Sweet-and-Sour Chicken Bowl
Royal Flavor

- 2 tablespoons frozen shelled edamame (soybeans)
- 1 teaspoon cornstarch
- 1/4 teaspoon garlic powder
- 1/8 teaspoon salt
- Black pepper to taste
- Pinch of cayenne
- 1 4-ounce boneless, skinless chicken breast, cut diagonally into 7-8 strips
- 1 teaspoon toasted sesame oil
- 1/4 cup 3/4-inch Royal Flavor* red bell pepper squares
- 1/4 cup 3/4-inch red onion squares
- 1 1/2 teaspoons minced garlic
- 1 tablespoon plus 2 teaspoons sweet-and-sour stir-fry sauce, divided
- 2/3 cup cooked whole-grain pilaf

Bring 2 cups salted water to a boil. Add edamame and cook for 5 minutes; drain well.

Mix cornstarch, garlic powder, salt, pepper and cayenne in a bowl. Add chicken and toss to coat.

Place a medium nonstick wok over high heat. Add sesame oil, edamame, peppers, onion and garlic. Cook until garlic softens, 1-2 minutes. Push veggies to the edges of the pan.

Add chicken in single layer in the center; cook until lightly browned then flip to the other side. Stir veggies, keeping them at the edges. When chicken is browned, mix in veggies and stir-fry until cooked to taste. Turn off heat and stir in 1 tablespoon sweet-and-sour sauce.

Place pilaf in a bowl. Top with remaining sauce and chicken mixture. Makes 1 serving.

Nutritional information: Each serving (1 bowl) has 500 calories, 38 g protein, 61 g carbohydrates, 11 g fat, 1 g saturated fat, 66 mg cholesterol, 10 g fiber, 413 mg sodium.

Recipe taken from Devin Alexander's The Most Decadent Diet Ever! *Copyright © 2008 by Devin Alexander published by Broadway Books, a division of Random House Inc.*
* Brands may vary by region; substitute a similar product.

Citrus Herb Roasted Chicken
Coleman Organic

- 1 Coleman* organic whole chicken (about 5 pounds) **Organic**
- 1 tablespoon Kirkland Signature Organic Dry Poultry Rub, divided **Organic**
- 2 oranges, peeled and quartered
- 1 small onion, coarsely chopped

HERB SEASONING TOPPING

- 2 garlic cloves, finely minced
- 2 shallots, finely minced
- 4 tablespoons extra-virgin olive oil
- 1 teaspoon finely ground sea salt
- 1 tablespoon Kirkland Signature Organic Dry Poultry Rub **Organic**

Preheat oven to 425°F.

Remove the giblet pack from inside the chicken cavity and save for use in soup or stock. Rinse chicken and pat dry. Rub inside of chicken with 1/2 tablespoon poultry rub. Combine orange quarters and onion with the remaining poultry rub and toss to coat evenly. Insert this mixture into the cavity.

Place chicken in a roasting pan, breast-side up.

To prepare the topping, combine the herb seasoning ingredients in a small bowl. Slide a small rubber spatula between the skin and the breast meat to separate. Spread half of the topping under the skin of both breasts from the cavity opening, spreading evenly over the whole breast area with the fingertips. Rub the remaining topping all over the outside of the bird.

Cover loosely with foil and bake for approximately 90 minutes, or until internal temperature is 165°F. Remove foil during the last 10 minutes of baking time to allow the chicken to brown.

Let stand for 5-10 minutes before carving. This allows all the natural juices to remain in the meat. Makes 4-6 servings.

Nutritional information: Each serving has 437 calories, 34 g protein, 12 g carbohydrates, 28 g fat, 7 g saturated fat, 105 mg cholesterol, 3 g fiber, 420 mg sodium.

* Brands may vary by region; substitute a similar product.

Citrus Walnut Pasta Salad
California Walnut Commission

3/4 cup coarsely chopped Kirkland Signature walnuts

3 cups (about 8 ounces) bow tie pasta (farfalle)

2 cups shredded cooked chicken (use rotisserie chicken from the Costco deli)

1 cup smoked cheese, such as Gouda, cut in 1/4-inch cubes

1 cup celery cut in thin diagonal slices

1/3 cup finely chopped red onion

3 tablespoons chopped fresh chives

2 tablespoons chopped fresh parsley

DRESSING

1/3 cup fresh orange juice

1/4 cup fresh lemon juice

4 tablespoons extra-virgin olive oil

1 tablespoon stone-ground mustard

2 teaspoons sugar

1 1/4 teaspoons salt

1/2 teaspoon freshly ground black pepper

2 teaspoons rice vinegar

Preheat oven to 350°F.

Place walnuts on a cookie sheet in a single layer and bake for 8-10 minutes, checking frequently. Let cool.

Cook pasta according to package directions. Drain and let cool completely.

To prepare the dressing, combine all ingredients in a large bowl, stirring with a whisk to blend.

Add pasta, chicken, cheese, celery, red onion, walnuts, chives and parsley to the dressing; toss gently to combine. Makes 6 servings.

Nutritional information: Each serving has 495 calories, 29 g protein, 37 g carbohydrates, 26 g fat, 6 g saturated fat, 62 mg cholesterol, 3 g fiber, 1,045 mg sodium.

Tips: If you buy walnuts in sealed packaging, they can be stored in their original packaging. Once you open the bag, transfer the walnuts to an airtight container to maintain freshness. Keep walnuts in an airtight container for up to six months in the refrigerator and up to one year in the freezer.

CALIFORNIA
Walnuts
www.walnuts.org

Grape Chutney
Kirschenman

Olive oil spray
$^1/_2$ cup finely chopped sweet onion
2 teaspoons minced garlic
1 cup chopped Kirschenman* red seedless grapes
$^1/_4$ cup chopped pitted green olives
$^1/_4$ cup dry white wine
2 teaspoons balsamic vinegar
Pinch of cinnamon, or more to taste
Salt and pepper

Place a medium nonstick saucepan over medium heat. Lightly mist the pan with spray and add onion and garlic. Cook for 5-7 minutes, or until onion and garlic soften.

Add grapes, olives, wine, vinegar and cinnamon, and increase the heat to medium-high. Simmer uncovered, stirring frequently, for 15-20 minutes, or until most of the liquid is absorbed. Season to taste with salt and pepper.

Serve immediately with chicken or fish. The chutney can also be stored in an airtight plastic container in the refrigerator for up to 3 days and then reheated. Makes 6 servings.

Nutritional information: Each 2-tablespoon serving has 35 calories, <1 g protein, 5 g carbohydrates, 1 g fat, trace saturated fat, 0 mg cholesterol, trace fiber, 93 mg sodium.

Recipe courtesy of Devin Alexander.
* Brands may vary by region; substitute a similar product.

Grilled Halibut and Grape Tomato Kabobs
Alpine Fresh

MARINADE
$^1/_2$ cup olive oil
2-3 garlic cloves, minced
$^1/_4$ cup minced onion
2 tablespoons (or 2 teaspoons dried) *each* chopped fresh basil, oregano and parsley
$^1/_4$ cup lemon juice

16 10-inch bamboo skewers
2 pounds halibut fillet
1 pound Alpine Fresh* grape tomatoes
1 large red onion, cut in $^1/_2$-inch wedges
1 large yellow bell pepper, cut in $^1/_2$-by-2-inch strips
1 large green bell pepper, cut in $^1/_2$-by-2-inch strips
Salt and pepper

Soak bamboo skewers in water for 1-2 hours.

To prepare the marinade, combine all ingredients in a glass bowl or gallon ziplock bag.

Cut halibut into small chunks. Place fish in the marinade and stir to coat. Cover and refrigerate for at least 1 hour. Remove halibut chunks from the marinade, reserving the marinade.

Assemble the skewers, alternating halibut, tomatoes, onion and peppers. Brush with the reserved marinade.

Grill over medium heat for 6-8 minutes, turning once, until the halibut is done. Season with salt and pepper to taste. Serve with rice pilaf or risotto, if desired. Makes 8 servings.

Nutritional information: Each serving has 279 calories, 25 g protein, 8 g carbohydrates, 16 g fat, 2 g saturated fat, 36 mg cholesterol, 2 g fiber, 67 mg sodium.

Recipe developed by Christine Jackson, food stylist.
* Brands may vary by region; substitute a similar product.

Grilled Salmon Parisian Salad
Ready Pac

1 16-ounce bag Ready Pac Grand Parisian salad mix

2 vine-ripe Roma tomatoes, cut in half and sliced

1 cup halved and thinly sliced seedless cucumber

3/4 cup halved and thinly sliced red onion

2 pounds wild salmon

3 tablespoons olive oil

1 tablespoon Kirkland Signature Herbed Seafood Rub

6 orange slices, cut in half (optional)

1 1/2 tablespoons capers, drained

Open the bag of salad and set topping and dressing packets aside. Place the lettuce blend with carrots in a chilled salad bowl; add tomatoes, cucumbers and red onions. Chill.

Cut salmon in 6 equal portions. Brush with olive oil. Sprinkle with seafood rub. Place on a hot grill, skin side down, about 4 inches directly above a hot fire. Cook until the flesh has turned from translucent to opaque, turning once, about 3-5 minutes on each side. Alternatively, place salmon on foil squares and top each with 2 orange slices. Fold foil to enclose. Grill foil-wrapped salmon on open flame for 5-7 minutes, or until cooked to taste.

Meanwhile, top chilled lettuce mixture with almonds, cranberries and feta cheese from the topping packets. Drizzle with the salad dressing and toss to mix.

To serve, arrange salad on chilled plates. Top with grilled salmon (hot or chilled). Sprinkle with capers. Makes 6 servings.

Nutritional information: Each serving has 327 calories, 35 g protein, 11 g carbohydrates, 16 g fat, 3 g saturated fat, 68 mg cholesterol, 3 g fiber, 477 mg sodium.

Fruit and Shrimp Kabobs
I.M. Ripe

1/4 cup extra-virgin olive oil

2 garlic cloves, minced

2 tablespoons chopped fresh herbs (such as basil, marjoram, rosemary and thyme)

1 I.M. Ripe peach, pitted

1 I.M. Ripe nectarine, pitted

1 I.M. Ripe plum, pitted

1 pound large peeled and deveined shrimp

1 lemon, halved and thinly sliced

Salt and freshly ground pepper

Heat olive oil in a small skillet until very hot. Add garlic and cook briefly until aromatic; do not allow the garlic to brown. Remove from the heat immediately and stir in herbs; set aside.

Cut peach, nectarine and plum into 1-inch chunks and thread onto skewers alternately with shrimp and lemon slices. Brush lightly with garlic-herb oil.

Grill over medium-high heat for 3-5 minutes per side, or until shrimp is pink and cooked through. Remove from the grill and drizzle with the remaining garlic-herb oil and salt and pepper to taste. Makes 5 servings.

Nutritional information: Each serving has 226 calories, 20 g protein, 9 g carbohydrates, 12 g fat, 2 g saturated fat, 177 mg cholesterol, 2 g fiber, 204 mg sodium.

Pan-Fried Salmon with Mango Cucumber Salsa
Alpine Fresh

MANGO CUCUMBER SALSA

6 tablespoons fresh lime juice

2 tablespoons honey

4 cups 1/4-inch cubes Alpine Fresh* whole or Alpine Fresh* sliced mangoes

3 cups 1/4-inch unpeeled hothouse (English) cucumber cubes

1 1/3 cups minced red onion

2 tablespoons minced and seeded green jalapeño pepper

Salt

1 teaspoon ground cumin

1/2 teaspoon salt, plus more to taste

Pinch of cayenne, plus more to taste (optional)

8 4-ounce salmon fillets, skin and bones removed

Olive oil spray

Black pepper (optional)

To prepare the salsa, whisk lime juice and honey in a medium resealable container until well combined. Add mango, cucumber, onion and jalapeño, and stir until well blended. Seal the container and refrigerate for at least 1 hour to let the flavors meld. Season with salt to taste. Serve cold or at room temperature.

To prepare the salmon, mix cumin, 1/2 teaspoon salt and pinch of cayenne in a small bowl. Lightly mist both sides of salmon fillets with spray. Sprinkle the spice mixture evenly over both sides.

Place a small nonstick skillet over medium-high heat. Cook the fillets until the outsides are just lightly browned, 1-2 minutes per side. Then lower the heat to medium and cook until the salmon is a pale pink throughout, 2-3 minutes per side.

Season with more salt, cayenne and black pepper to taste, if desired. Transfer each fillet to a plate. Top each with half of the salsa. Makes 8 servings.

Nutritional information: Each serving (1 fillet with salsa) has 201 calories, 23 g protein, 10 g carbohydrates, 7 g fat, 1 g saturated fat, 62 mg cholesterol, 1 g fiber, 212 mg sodium.

Recipe by Devin Alexander from The Most Decadent Diet Ever!
* Brands may vary by region; substitute a similar product.

Hawaiian Island Niçoise Salad
Norpac Fisheries Export

1 teaspoon salmon and seafood seasoning

1 8-ounce Hawaiian Select* fresh or frozen ahi steak

1 tablespoon olive oil

6-8 ounces organic spring mix

2 new potatoes, cooked and sliced

5-10 kalamata olives

3 ounces fresh green beans, blanched

1 ounce red onion, julienned

2 tomatoes, quartered

1 hard-boiled egg, coarsely chopped

DRESSING

1/4 cup red wine vinegar

1/4 cup olive oil

Sea salt

Coarsely grated black peppercorns

Sprinkle seasoning over ahi. Heat olive oil in a sauté pan over medium heat. Add ahi and sear for 1 1/2 minutes on each side.

To prepare the dressing, pour vinegar into a small mixing bowl. While whisking continuously, slowly drizzle olive oil into the vinegar until emulsified. Season to taste with salt and pepper.

To assemble, add spring mix to the dressing and toss. Arrange in the center of a large plate or bowl. Place potatoes, olives, beans, onions, tomatoes and egg in a row around the edge of the greens. Top the greens with the seared ahi. Makes 1-2 servings.

Nutritional information: Each serving has 645 calories, 19 g protein, 38 g carbohydrates, 42 g fat, 6 g saturated fat, 189 mg cholesterol, 9 g fiber, 810 mg sodium.

* Brands may vary by region; substitute a similar product.

Contemporary Peppered Chopped Steak
Kirkland Signature/Newman's Own

4 ounces 96% lean ground beef

3 tablespoons cooked brown rice (white rice works in a pinch)

5 teaspoons minced fresh parsley, divided

1/8 teaspoon salt

1 teaspoon freshly ground black pepper

Olive oil spray

1/2 cup thin sweet onion rings

1/3 cup Kirkland Signature/Newman's Own 100% Grape Juice

1 tablespoon balsamic vinegar

In a medium bowl, mix beef, rice, 4 teaspoons parsley and salt until well combined. Form into a 1-inch-thick oval patty. Season with pepper, pressing it into the patty on all sides.

Place a small nonstick skillet over high heat. When it's hot, lightly mist the skillet with spray and add the patty. Cook for 2-4 minutes per side, or until the outside browns and the inside is very slightly less done than desired. Place the steak on a plate and cover to keep warm.

Reduce the heat to medium and respray the pan. Add onions and cook for about 5 minutes, or until tender. Add grape juice and vinegar and return the heat to high. Boil for 4-5 minutes, or until only about 1/4 cup of the liquid remains.

Spoon the onions and sauce over the steak. Sprinkle with remaining parsley. Serve immediately. Makes 1 serving.

Nutritional information: Each serving has 275 calories, 24 g protein, 32 g carbohydrates, 6 g fat, 2 g saturated fat, 60 mg cholesterol, 3 g fiber, 372 mg sodium.

Recipe adapted from The Biggest Loser Family Cookbook by Chef Devin Alexander and The Biggest Loser experts and cast with Melissa Roberson.

Fruit Kebabs with Cinnamon Cream
Divine Flavor

8 wooden skewers
8 Divine Flavor* red or green seedless grapes
8 1 1/2-inch watermelon cubes
8 1 1/2-inch cantaloupe cubes
8 1 1/2-inch pineapple cubes
8 strawberries, trimmed
1/4 teaspoon ground cinnamon
1/2 cup nonfat vanilla yogurt

On each skewer, place 1 grape, then 1 watermelon cube, 1 cantaloupe cube, 1 pineapple cube and 1 strawberry. Arrange on a serving platter.

Mix cinnamon with yogurt. Serve the fruit kebabs with cinnamon cream for dipping. Makes 4 servings.

Nutritional information: Each serving has 66 calories, 2 g protein, 16 g carbohydrates, trace fat, trace saturated fat, <1 mg cholesterol, 1 g fiber, 24 mg sodium.

Recipe courtesy of Devin Alexander.
* Brands may vary by region; substitute a similar product.

DIVINE FLAVOR

World-Famous Fruit Trifle
Stemilt Growers

1 8-ounce carton Stemilt*
fresh blueberries

2 large fresh, ripe Stemilt*
pears (Anjou or Bartlett)

1 small lemon

3-4 large fresh, ripe Stemilt*
peaches or nectarines

1 cup (about 8 ounces) fresh
Stemilt* cherries

8-10 ounces Greek-style
yogurt with honey
(see note)

1 fresh Stemilt* apple
(Fuji, Pink Lady or other
sweet variety)

Select a large clear-glass vase or trifle dish for the trifle. Any dramatic shape will work, but the opening should be the same diameter as or wider than the base, for ease in serving.

Wash blueberries and pat dry. Layer on the bottom of the vase, reserving a few.

Peel, core and cut pears into bite-size pieces. Place in a bowl and sprinkle with juice from half of the lemon, stirring to coat well. Layer pears on top of the blueberries in the vase.

Peel and chop peaches or nectarines into bite-size chunks. Place in a layer on top of the pears.

Wash cherries; reserve a few whole ones for garnish and remove stems and pits from the others. If you don't have a cherry pitter, cut cherries in half and pop out the seeds. Layer the pitted cherries on top of the peaches.

Just before serving, spread a layer of yogurt on top of the fruit.

Wash and core apple, cut a few slices and sprinkle with lemon juice. Arrange the apple slices in a "fan" garnish on the trifle. Top with the reserved cherries and blueberries. Makes 6 servings.

Nutritional information: Each serving has 165 calories, 4 g protein, 38 g carbohydrates, 2 g fat, <1 g saturated fat, 5 mg cholesterol, 6 g fiber, 28 mg sodium.

Note: Greek-style yogurt is made from whole milk, so it has a denser texture than traditional yogurt. It is often sold with honey, or you can add it yourself—about 1 table-spoon per 5 ounces, just enough to sweeten. If Greek-style yogurt is not available, substitute whole-milk yogurt. Choose a plain flavor such as vanilla for best results.

Tip: To prepare individual servings, divide the fruit and layer in wine glasses or parfait dishes. The amount of fruit suggested can be adjusted to accommodate the size of the dish or the group being served.

* Brands may vary by region; substitute a similar product.

On-the-Terrace Fruit Salad
Unifrutti of America

1 24-ounce jar red
grapefruit in slightly
sweetened juice or
in its own juice (not
in syrup)

2 cups bite-sized fresh
(not canned)
pineapple chunks

1 1/2 cups bite-sized,
peeled kiwi chunks

1 cup bite-sized
strawberry pieces

1 cup bite-sized
cantaloupe chunks

2 cups bite-sized red
apple chunks

Mint leaves, for garnish

Pour grapefruit, juice included, into a large glass or plastic mixing bowl. Add pineapple, kiwi, strawberries, cantaloupe and apples. Stir gently to combine.

Spoon 1 cup of the fruit along with some of the juice into each of 9 white wine glasses or bowls. Serve immediately, or refrigerate for up to 2 days. Garnish with mint, if desired. Makes about 9 servings.

Nutritional information: Each 1-cup serving has 97 calories, <1 g protein, 24 g carbohydrates, <1 g fat, trace saturated fat, 0 mg cholesterol, 3 g fiber, 14 mg sodium.

Tip: Regular grapefruit can be substituted for red grapefruit. But steer clear of the ones in syrup. You really don't need the added sugar.

Recipe by Devin Alexander from The Most Decadent Diet Ever!

Grape Granita
Four Star Fruit

2 cups Four Star Fruit red
    seedless grapes, frozen
2 teaspoons honey

Place frozen grapes and honey in a food processor fitted with a chopping blade. Process the ingredients, scraping down the bowl of the processor if necessary, until the grapes are very finely chopped and mostly smooth in texture.

Divide into 2 martini glasses or dessert bowls. Serve immediately. Makes 2 servings.

Nutritional information: Each heaping $3/4$-cup serving has 81 calories, <1 g protein, 22 g carbohydrates, <1 g fat, 0 mg saturated fat, 0 mg cholesterol, <1 g fiber, trace sodium.

Recipe from The Biggest Loser Family Cookbook *by Chef Devin Alexander and* The Biggest Loser *experts and cast with Melissa Roberson.*

Peach Shortcake
Fowler Packing

**BETTER BUTTERMILK
BISCUITS**

Butter-flavored
    cooking spray
$3/4$ cup plus 3 tablespoons
    unbleached all-purpose
    flour, plus more
    for dusting
$1/2$ cup whole-wheat
    pastry flour
1 teaspoon sugar
1 teaspoon baking powder
$1/2$ teaspoon salt
$1/2$ teaspoon baking soda
3 tablespoons cold
    light butter (stick,
    not tub), cut into pieces
$2/3$ cup low-fat
    buttermilk
1 large egg
4 ripe peaches
1 $1/2$ cups fat-free frozen
    whipped topping,
    defrosted, divided

To make the biscuits, preheat the oven to 400°F. Lightly spray an 11-by-7-inch ovenproof glass or ceramic baking dish.

Combine dry biscuit ingredients in a medium mixing bowl. Cut in the butter until crumbly. Add the buttermilk. Stir with a fork just until moistened.

On a lightly floured work surface, knead the dough gently, adding a little flour until the dough forms a ball. Pat the ball into a $1/2$-inch-thick rectangle.

Cut 6 biscuits with a floured 3-inch round biscuit cutter or cookie cutter; transfer them to the prepared dish about $3/4$ inch apart. Beat the egg with 1 tablespoon water in a small bowl. Lightly brush the top of each biscuit with the egg mixture.

Bake for 13-15 minutes, or until lightly golden on top. Cool for a few minutes on a rack. Cut the biscuits in half horizontally. Place the bottom half of each biscuit on a dessert plate.

Peel the peaches and cut them into $1/4$-inch-thick half-moons. Divide evenly among the biscuits. Top each with $1/4$ cup whipped topping. Then rest the biscuit tops on an angle to one side of each. Serve immediately. Makes 6 servings.

Nutritional information: Each serving has 201 calories, 6 g protein, 37 g carbohydrates, 4 g fat, 2 g saturated fat, 18 mg cholesterol, 2 g fiber, 456 mg sodium.

Recipe by Devin Alexander from The Most Decadent Diet Ever!

Breakfast

Cherry and Apple Crêpes
Primavera

2 pounds Prima Frutta*
   fresh cherries, halved
   and pitted (about
   3 cups)

3 medium Crystal Market*
   California apples, peeled
   and diced (about 2 cups)

1/4 cup Grand
   Marnier liqueur

2 tablespoons cornstarch

1/2 cup water

2 tablespoons butter

1/2 cup sugar

1 teaspoon vanilla extract

1/2 teaspoon
   almond extract

1 package prepared
   crêpes (10 6-inch
   square work best)

2 cups sweetened
   whipped cream

1 cup chopped Prima
   Noce* walnuts

Combine cherries and apples in a small bowl; set aside.

In another bowl, combine Grand Marnier, cornstarch and water, stirring until well blended.

In a 4-quart saucepan, melt butter, then stir in sugar. Add cornstarch mixture and heat, stirring constantly, over medium-high until hot. Add 3 cups of the cherry-apple mixture and bring to a simmer. Reduce heat and cook until thickened. Remove from the heat and stir in vanilla and almond extract; set aside.

Place 2 tablespoons of the warm fruit mixture in the center of each crêpe. Fold the corners in toward the middle.

Add the remaining cherries and apples to the fruit mixture and stir. Do not cook. Spoon 1 tablespoon of the fruit mixture on top of each crêpe. Top with whipped cream, drizzle 1 teaspoon of the sauce over the whipped cream and sprinkle with walnuts. Serve immediately. Makes 10 crêpes.

* Brands may vary by region; substitute a similar product.

Crespelle con i Fichi
(Crêpes with Figs)
Catania Worldwide

12 fresh figs

2 tablespoons dark rum

1/3 cup confectioners'
   sugar, divided

1 cup heavy cream

CRÊPES

1 cup all-purpose flour

2 eggs

1/2 cup milk

1/2 cup water

1/4 teaspoon salt

2 tablespoons
   butter, melted

Cooking oil

Rinse figs and dry well. Cut each fig into 4 wedges. Place the figs in a skillet and sprinkle with rum and 2 tablespoons confectioners' sugar. Cover and cook over low heat for 10 minutes. Remove from the heat.

Whip the cream.

To prepare the crêpes, whisk together flour and eggs in a large mixing bowl. Gradually add milk and water, stirring to combine. Add salt and butter; beat until smooth.

Heat a lightly oiled griddle or frying pan over medium-high heat. For each crêpe, pour or scoop 1/4 cup batter onto the griddle, tilting the pan with a circular motion to coat the surface evenly. Cook for about 2 minutes, or until the bottom is light brown. Loosen with a spatula, turn and cook the other side.

Spread the fig mixture over the hot crêpes. Roll up loosely. Sprinkle with the remaining confectioners' sugar. Serve with whipped cream. Makes 4 servings.

German Apple Pancake
Krusteaz

APPLE TOPPING
1/4 cup butter or margarine

2 cups peeled, thinly
sliced apples

1/4 cup sugar

1/2 teaspoon ground
cinnamon

PANCAKE BATTER
1 cup Krusteaz Buttermilk
Complete Pancake Mix

3/4 cup water

1/2 teaspoon vanilla extract

1/2 teaspoon ground
cinnamon

To prepare the topping, place butter in a 9-inch microwave-safe pie pan. Microwave on high for 45-60 seconds, or until butter is melted. Stir in apples, sugar and cinnamon. Cover and microwave on high for 3-4 minutes, or until apples are tender.

To prepare the batter, place pancake mix, water, vanilla and cinnamon in a medium bowl and blend with a wire whisk. Pour evenly over the cooked apples.

Microwave, uncovered, on high for 3-5 minutes, or until a toothpick inserted in the center comes out clean. Let stand for 3-5 minutes, then invert onto a serving plate. Optional serving suggestion: Sprinkle with additional cinnamon and confectioners' sugar. Makes 6-8 servings.

Tip: To use a conventional oven, preheat to 350°F. Prepare apple topping as directed. Bake, uncovered, for 10 minutes, or until apples are tender. Prepare pancake batter and pour evenly over the cooked apples. Bake, uncovered, for 13-15 minutes, or until a toothpick inserted in the center comes out clean.

KRUSTEAZ

Banana-Carrot Loaf (Low-Fat)
Tree Top

Nonfat cooking spray

3/4 cup All-Natural Tree
Top* apple sauce

1 cup sugar

2 eggs or 4 egg whites

1 3/4 cups flour

1 teaspoon salt

3/4 teaspoon baking soda

1 teaspoon baking powder

1 teaspoon ground
cinnamon

1 cup grated carrots

1 cup mashed bananas
(about 3)

Preheat oven to 350°F. Coat a 9-by-5-inch loaf pan with cooking spray.

In a medium-sized mixing bowl, combine apple sauce, sugar and eggs; beat until light and fluffy.

In a separate bowl, combine flour, salt, baking soda, baking powder and cinnamon. Add to the batter and blend well.

Fold carrots and bananas into the batter.

Pour batter into the prepared pan. Bake for 60-65 minutes, or until a toothpick inserted in the center comes out clean. Makes 10 servings.

Tip: Dust lightly with confectioners' sugar or spread with whipped low-fat cream cheese and chopped nuts.

Brands may vary by region; substitute a similar product.

Banana-Nutella Stuffed Croissant
Vie de France

1 large Vie de France butter croissant

4 tablespoons cream cheese, softened

2 tablespoons Nutella

1/2 banana, sliced into rounds

3 tablespoons granulated brown sugar

1 egg

1/4 cup milk

2 tablespoons sugar

1 tablespoon rum

1/2 teaspoon vanilla extract

Butter

Confectioners' sugar (optional)

Fresh fruit (optional)

Slice croissant lengthwise almost all the way through. Spread cream cheese on both sides. Spread Nutella on top of cream cheese.

Toss banana slices with brown sugar and place in an ovenproof pan. Put under a hot broiler for about 30 seconds, or until the sugar melts. Place banana slices on top of Nutella and close the croissant.

In a bowl, combine egg, milk, sugar, rum and vanilla; mix until well blended. Dunk the croissant into the batter, soaking well.

Heat a sauté pan over medium heat and coat with a little butter. Add the croissant and cook like French toast, turning once. Top with confectioners' sugar and fresh fruit, if desired. Makes 1 serving.

Asparagus, Bell Pepper and Basil Egg Tart
Kirkland Signature/Michael Foods

1/3 cup cold butter, cut into small pieces

1 cup all-purpose flour

2-3 tablespoons cold water

1 cup shredded Cheddar cheese

1/2 pound asparagus spears, cut into 2-inch pieces

1/2 medium red bell pepper, cut into thin strips

1/4 cup chopped fresh basil

1 cup (8 ounces) Kirkland Signature* Egg Starts

1 cup half-and-half

1/4 teaspoon salt

1/8 teaspoon ground pepper

2 tablespoons pine nuts

Preheat oven to 450°F.

With a pastry blender, cut butter into flour until the mixture resembles coarse crumbs. Slowly add cold water until the dough forms a ball. On a lightly floured surface, roll the dough into a 12-inch circle. Press into an ungreased 10-inch tart pan with a removable bottom. Line the crust with aluminum foil and pie weights. Bake for 8 minutes, or until lightly browned.

Reduce oven temperature to 400°F.

Sprinkle the crust with cheese. Top with asparagus, bell pepper and basil.

In a bowl, combine Egg Starts, half-and-half, salt and pepper. Pour over the vegetables. Top with pine nuts.

Bake for 30-35 minutes, or until set in the center. Makes 8-10 servings.

Tip: Dried beans can be used for pie weights.

Brands may vary by region; substitute a similar product.

Breakfast Casserole
Jimmy Dean

1 pound Regular Flavor Jimmy Dean* Pork Sausage

10 eggs, lightly beaten

3 cups milk

2 teaspoons dry mustard

1 teaspoon salt

6 cups cubed bread

1/2 teaspoon ground black pepper

2 cups shredded sharp Cheddar cheese

1/2 cup sliced mushrooms (optional)

1 medium tomato, seeded and chopped (optional)

1/2 cup thinly sliced green onions (optional)

Preheat oven to 325°F.

In a large skillet, cook sausage over medium-high heat, stirring frequently, until thoroughly cooked and no longer pink.

In a large mixing bowl, combine eggs, milk, mustard and salt; stir well.

Distribute half the bread cubes evenly in a buttered 13-by-9-by-2-inch baking dish. Sprinkle with half the pepper, half the cheese, half the sausage and half of each optional ingredient. Repeat layering using remaining bread cubes, pepper, cheese, sausage and optional ingredients. Pour the egg mixture evenly over the casserole.

Bake, uncovered, for 55-60 minutes, or until the eggs are set. Tent with foil if the top begins to brown too quickly. Makes 6 servings.

Brands may vary by region; substitute a similar product.

Hearty Egg Casserole

Norco Ranch/Nucal Foods/Cal-Maine Foods/Zephyr Egg/Wilcox Farms/ Hillandale Farms/Oakdell Egg Farms/ Hickman's Family Farms

Cooking spray

1 28-ounce package frozen Southern-style hash brown potatoes, about 6 cups

1 8-ounce package shredded sharp Cheddar cheese (2 cups)

10 eggs, well beaten

1 cup reduced-fat sour cream

1 cup skim or low-fat milk

2 tablespoons honey Dijon mustard (optional)

1 teaspoon salt

1/4 teaspoon ground pepper

Sliced red onion (optional)

Parsley sprig (optional)

Mixed greens (optional)

Preheat oven to 350°F. Evenly coat a 13-by-9-inch (3 quart) glass baking dish with cooking spray.

Evenly spread potatoes in the dish. Sprinkle with cheese.

In a large bowl, beat together eggs, sour cream, milk, mustard, salt and pepper until thoroughly blended. Pour over the potatoes.

Bake until puffed and browned and no visible liquid egg remains, about 45 minutes.

Garnish with onion and parsley. Serve with mixed greens, if desired. Makes 8 servings.

Flax and Carrot Muffins
Nature's Path Organic Foods

2 large eggs or egg substitute

1 cup well-shaken buttermilk

3/4 cup packed dark brown sugar

2 teaspoons vanilla extract

1 1/2 cups Nature's Path Flax Plus Multibran Cereal **Organic**

1 1/4 cups whole-wheat pastry flour

2 teaspoons baking powder

1/2 teaspoon baking soda

3/4 teaspoon ground cinnamon

1/4 teaspoon salt

1/3 cup vegetable oil

1 1/2 cups grated carrots (4 medium carrots)

1/2 cup chopped walnuts

1/3 cup dried currants

Set rack in center of oven and preheat oven to 375°F. Place paper liners in 12 standard muffin cups.

In a large bowl, lightly beat eggs. Blend in buttermilk, brown sugar and vanilla. Add cereal, crushing the flakes in your hands as you go. Stir well and set aside.

In another bowl, combine flour, baking powder, baking soda, cinnamon and salt.

Stir oil, carrots, walnuts and currants into the buttermilk mixture. Add the dry ingredients and stir just until the flour is absorbed. Do not overmix.

Divide the batter among prepared muffin cups. Bake for 10 minutes. Rotate the pan and continue baking until a toothpick inserted in the center comes out clean, 10-12 more minutes. Makes 12 muffins.

Cherry Almond Scones
Morada Produce

2 cups self-rising flour

2 tablespoons sugar

1/2 teaspoon salt

6 tablespoons butter, chilled

1/2 cup buttermilk

2 eggs, divided

1 1/2 cups quartered and pitted Morada Produce* fresh cherries

ALMOND GLAZE

1 cup confectioners' sugar

2-3 tablespoons milk

1 teaspoon almond extract

1/2 cup slivered almonds, toasted

Preheat oven to 400°F.

In a bowl, combine flour, sugar and salt. Cut in butter with fingertips to the size of small peas.

In another bowl, whisk together buttermilk and 1 egg. Fold into the dry ingredients just until moistened. Stir in cherries gently.

Using a medium-sized ice cream scoop, scoop scones onto a parchment-lined pan, spacing evenly.

Beat remaining egg, then brush over the scones. Bake for 15-20 minutes, or until a toothpick inserted in the center comes out clean. Let cool on a rack.

To prepare the glaze, place sugar, milk and almond extract in a small bowl and stir until blended.

Brush the glaze over the scones and sprinkle with toasted almonds. Makes 6-8 servings.

Brands may vary by region; substitute a similar product.

Easy and Fast Breakfast Energy Bar Poppers
Kirkland Signature/ Cranberry Macadamia Cereal

1 cup honey

1 cup sugar

1 teaspoon kosher salt

1 teaspoon pure vanilla extract

1 cup extra-crunchy peanut butter

1 17-ounce pouch Kirkland Signature Cranberry Macadamia cereal

In a microwave, heat honey, sugar and salt to a full rolling boil.

Remove and stir in vanilla and peanut butter, blending until smooth.

Pour over cereal until evenly coated.

When the mixture is cool enough to handle but still very warm, roll tablespoons of dough into balls. (Option: To make bars, firmly press the mixture into a 13-by-9-inch pan heavily coated with cooking spray.)

Let cool for 30-40 minutes. Cover and store for an easy on-the-go breakfast or snack. Makes 24 servings.

Taquito Brunch Skillet
El Monterey

2 tablespoons olive oil or butter

2 cups potatoes cut in $1/2$-inch cubes, fresh or precooked

1 cup fresh diced onions

10 El Monterey beef or chicken taquitos, thawed and diced in $1/2$-inch pieces

$1/2$ cup diced tomatoes

$1/2$ cup diced celery

$1/2$ cup La Victoria Thick'N Chunky red salsa

$1/4$ cup diced black olives

2 eggs

1 cup 3-cheese shredded Mexican blend

Fried onion topping, bacon bits or chopped fresh cilantro (optional)

Heat oil in a large skillet over medium-high heat.

Add potatoes and onions; fry for 2 minutes, or until potatoes are soft and onions are translucent.

Add diced taquitos, tomatoes, celery, salsa and black olives. Cook until heated through.

Break eggs into a bowl and whisk. Add cheese to the bowl and mix well. Pour the mixture into the skillet.

Cook until the eggs are done. Serve immediately, garnished with fried onions, bacon bits or chopped cilantro. Makes 4-6 servings.

Tip: For variety, crack whole eggs on top of the hot skillet mixture and cover to cook eggs sunny side up.

Appetizers

Granny Smith Apple Salsa
Domex Superfresh Growers

1 large tomato, cored and finely chopped

¾ cup finely chopped sweet onion

3 tablespoons freshly squeezed lime juice

1 large jalapeño chile, cored, seeded and finely chopped

2 Superfresh Growers* Granny Smith apples

2 tablespoons minced fresh cilantro

1 tablespoon honey

Salt and freshly ground black pepper

Corn chips

Stir together tomato, onion, lime juice and jalapeño in a medium bowl.

Quarter and core apples and cut into fine dice. Stir apples into the tomato mixture with cilantro, honey, and salt and pepper to taste.

Refrigerate for up to 6 hours before serving.

To serve, spoon the salsa into a serving bowl and place a bowl of corn chips alongside.

Makes 6-8 servings.

Brands may vary by region; substitute a similar product.

Toasted Jalapeño, Tomatillo and Watermelon Salsa
Timco Worldwide

8-10 medium tomatillos, parchment-like coating removed, rinsed

2 tablespoons vegetable oil

1 onion, minced

2 garlic cloves, minced

3 jalapeño peppers or to taste, seeded and chopped

1 tablespoon ground cumin

2 teaspoons mild chili powder

1 cup tomato sauce or purée

1 cup watermelon chunks

Salt and pepper to taste

Cut tomatillos into quarters.

Heat oil in a large heavy sauté pan over medium-high heat. Add onion and sauté for a few minutes. Add tomatillos, garlic and jalapeños. Sauté until the onions and garlic begin to brown.

Reduce the heat to low and sprinkle cumin and chili powder over the pan. Stir in tomato sauce and bring to a simmer. Remove from the heat and let cool.

Place the mixture in a blender or food processor. Add watermelon and purée. Season to taste with salt and pepper. Makes about 3 cups.

Game Time Mexican Dip
Fresherized Foods

1 tablespoon butter

1 small red bell pepper, chopped (1/2 cup)

1 medium onion, chopped (1/2 cup)

2 15-ounce cans black beans, rinsed and drained

1-2 teaspoons freshly chopped jalapeño pepper

1/2 teaspoon ground cumin

1 cup salsa

2 cups shredded Cheddar or Colby cheese

12 ounces Wholly Guacamole*

1/2 cup sour cream

1 bag tortilla chips

Melt butter in a 10-inch skillet until sizzling; add bell pepper and onion. Cook over medium heat, stirring occasionally, for 3-5 minutes, or until onion is softened. Stir in beans, jalapeños and cumin. Continue cooking for 2-3 minutes, or until heated through.

Transfer 1 cup of the bean mixture to a food processor, cover and process on high until smooth, approximately 30 seconds. Return the blended mixture to the remaining bean mixture and stir to combine. Spread the bean mixture in an 11-by-8-inch baking dish. Cover and refrigerate for 2 hours or overnight.

Just before serving, layer salsa, cheese and guacamole over the bean mixture.

Spoon sour cream into a resealable plastic food bag. Snip off the corner and pipe sour cream over the guacamole to resemble yard lines on a football field.

Serve with tortilla chips. Makes 15 servings.

* Brands may vary by region; substitute a similar product.

Summer Salsa
Don Miguel Mexican Foods

1/2 red onion, chopped or diced

2 serrano peppers, diced

1 peach, diced

1 mango, diced

1 cup diced papaya

1/4 cup chopped fresh cilantro

Salt and pepper to taste

Combine all ingredients and stir to blend.

For best results, cover and refrigerate overnight. Makes 8-10 servings.

Tip: Serve with any Don Miguel* Mexican appetizer items. This is also a fantastic addition to the Don Miguel Lean Ole Burrito, creating a light summer meal or snack.

* Brands may vary by region; substitute a similar product.

Cowboy Caviar
Eurofresh Farms

- 1 15-ounce can shoepeg corn, drained
- 1 15-ounce can black-eyed peas, drained
- 1 avocado, peeled and diced
- 2/3 cup cilantro, chopped
- 2-3 green onions, chopped
- 3-4 Eurofresh Farms* Roma Tomatoes on the Vine, chopped
- 1/4 cup olive oil
- 1/4 cup red wine vinegar
- 2 garlic cloves, crushed
- 3/4 teaspoon salt
- 1/8 teaspoon ground pepper
- 1 tablespoon ground cumin

In a medium bowl, combine corn, black-eyed peas, avocado, cilantro, green onions and tomatoes.

In a small bowl, whisk together olive oil, vinegar, garlic, salt, pepper and cumin. Add to the vegetable mixture and toss to coat.

Serve with tortilla chips or toasted pita chips. Makes 4-6 servings.

Brands may vary by region; substitute a similar product.

EURO
FRESH
FARMS
GARDEN FRESH FLAVOR

Asparagus-Prosciutto Rolls
Cabot Creamery

12 asparagus spears
4 large (14- by 18-inch) sheets phyllo dough, thawed
4 tablespoons Cabot* salted butter, melted
12 thin slices prosciutto
12 thin slices Cabot* 3 Year Old Cheddar or Vintage Choice Cheddar

Preheat oven to 375°F. Have a bowl of ice water on hand.

In a pot of boiling, salted water, cook asparagus for 1 minute. Transfer to the ice water with a slotted spoon. Once cool, transfer to paper towels to drain; pat dry.

Lay the first phyllo sheet on a cutting board; brush the entire surface with melted butter. Top with the next phyllo sheet and brush with butter; repeat with remaining 2 sheets. Cut into 12 rectangles.

Place 1 piece of prosciutto and Cheddar on each rectangle. Place asparagus spears on top with tips extending beyond the edges. Roll phyllo up around asparagus and brush with additional butter.

Place the rolls on a baking sheet and bake for 10-12 minutes, or until golden. Serve warm.
Makes 12 servings.

Brands may vary by region; substitute a similar product.

Fire-Roasted Sunset Ancient Sweet Pepper Rounds with Herb and Citrus Goat Cheese
Mastronardi Produce/Sunset

10 small Sunset Ancient Sweet Peppers
16 ounces soft goat cheese
10 ounces cream cheese (not whipped)
Finely grated peel of 1 orange
Juice of 1/2 lemon
1 bunch chives, chopped
Salt and white pepper

Over an open flame or with a small blowtorch, quickly blister and char the skin of the peppers. Submerge in iced water to stop the cooking. Remove the charred skin under cold running water. Pat dry.

Cut the tops off the peppers and remove the seeds, keeping the peppers whole. Drain if necessary. Set in the refrigerator on paper towels to absorb excess moisture.

In a mixing bowl, blend cheeses, grated orange peel, lemon juice and chives gently with a wooden spoon. Season to taste with salt and pepper.

With a rubber spatula, transfer the cheese mixture to a piping bag with a 1/2-inch round tip. Insert the piping bag into each chilled pepper as far as possible and pipe cheese evenly into the pepper, pulling out as it fills.

Refrigerate the filled peppers until the cheese is firm. Then slice into 1/2-inch rounds with a very sharp knife. Do this gently and quickly so as not to misshape and soften the filling. Chill until serving.
Makes 10 servings.

Goodness Grown Naturally™

Spinach Arancini
Kirkland Signature/Request Foods

When serving Kirkland Signature frozen lasagna, start the meal with this appetizer.

1/4 cup extra-virgin olive oil
1 cup minced onion
3 tablespoons minced garlic
1 1/2 cups Arborio rice
1 cup white wine
4 cups vegetable broth, heated
1 1/2 cups grated Parmigiano-
    Reggiano cheese
2 cups frozen chopped spinach
2 tablespoons unsalted butter

3 tablespoons chopped fresh basil
Salt
Ground black pepper
1 cup all-purpose flour
3/4 teaspoon cayenne pepper
3 eggs, beaten
2 cups Japanese bread crumbs
    (panko)
Canola oil

Heat olive oil in a 2-quart saucepan over medium heat. Add onions and garlic and sauté for about 5 minutes.

Add rice and wine; cook until liquid is reduced. Add broth by thirds, reducing each time until the mixture thickens.

Stir in grated cheese, spinach and butter. Then add basil and salt and pepper to taste.

Place in a container and let cool. Cover and refrigerate for 8-24 hours.

In a shallow bowl, combine flour and cayenne, stirring to mix well. Place eggs and bread crumbs in separate bowls.

Roll the spinach mixture into 1-inch balls. Dip balls in flour, then egg and then bread crumbs. Place on a cookie sheet.

In a large heavy pan, heat 1/4 inch of canola oil to 350°F. Fry the spinach balls until golden brown. Remove and place on a paper-towel-lined cookie sheet to drain. Serve hot. Makes 10-12 servings.

Tip: Arancini can be served with roasted red pepper aioli, chipotle sauce or sun-dried tomato sauce.

KIRKLAND Signature   **R REQUEST FOODS**

Grilled Asparagus Wrapped in Prosciutto
Alpine Fresh

4 ounces thinly sliced prosciutto di Parma

16 Alpine Fresh* asparagus spears, trimmed

Kosher salt

Freshly cracked black pepper

ORANGE AIOLI

1/2 cup orange juice

Grated zest of 1 orange

1 garlic clove, chopped

1 tablespoon finely chopped shallots

1 teaspoon cayenne pepper

2 large eggs

2 large egg yolks

2 1/2 cups olive oil

1 tablespoon kosher salt

Freshly cracked black pepper

Separate and lay out prosciutto slices on a flat surface. Lay an asparagus spear on a slight diagonal on the bottom of each slice and roll, covering as much of the stalk as possible and leaving the tip visible. Sprinkle with salt and pepper to taste. Place on a small baking sheet. Cover and refrigerate for 1 hour.

To prepare the aioli, combine orange juice, zest, garlic, shallots, cayenne, eggs and egg yolks in the bowl of a small food processor. Process until the ingredients are blended. With the processor running, slowly drizzle in olive oil, blending until the mixture is emulsified. Season with salt and pepper to taste. Chill for about 30 minutes.

Preheat a gas grill or prepare a fire in a charcoal grill.

Place the asparagus on the grill and cook, turning occasionally, until it is just tender and the prosciutto is crisped, about 4-6 minutes. If the prosciutto browns before the asparagus is cooked, move the spears to a cooler part of the grill.

Arrange the asparagus on plates and spoon aioli over them. Place the remaining aioli in a bowl for dipping. Makes 4 servings.

Recipe by Marsha M. Carter.
* Brands may vary by region; substitute a similar product.

Provençal Roasted Olives
Lindsay Olives

1 pint (2 cups) grape or cherry tomatoes

1 cup Lindsay black ripe olives

1 cup Lindsay kalamata pitted olives

1 cup Lindsay garlic-stuffed Spanish olives

1 tablespoon herbes de Provence blend *or* a mix of rosemary and thyme

8 whole garlic cloves, peeled

1/4 cup olive oil

1/4 teaspoon freshly ground black pepper

Toasted baguette slices or crackers

Preheat oven to 425°F.

Lay out tomatoes, olives, herbs, garlic, olive oil and pepper on a sheet pan and toss to combine well. Roast for 15-20 minutes, or until the tomatoes have shriveled and browned lightly. Let cool on the sheet pan, then transfer to a shallow bowl.

Serve at room temperature with toasted baguette slices or crackers. Makes 8 servings.

Note: Herbes de Provence is a dried herbal blend that typically contains rosemary, fennel, marjoram, basil, sage, thyme, summer savory and lavender. If you can't find it, make your own mix of a few of the designated dried herbs that you have on your pantry shelf. It will be delicious.

Tips: If you don't have the specified olives, feel free to use any combination. Fresh herbs such as rosemary, thyme and basil look great as a garnish.

Bagel Chips with Spinach Artichoke Cream Cheese Dip

Einstein Brothers Bagels/Noah's Bagels

3 tablespoons extra-virgin olive oil

1 teaspoon dried thyme

1 teaspoon dried oregano

1/2 teaspoon kosher salt
(or 1/4 teaspoon regular salt)

1/4 teaspoon coarsely ground
black pepper

4 Kirkland Signature plain bagels,
cut into 1/4-inch wedges

DIP

2 tubs (12 ounces) Einstein Bros.
or Noah's Plain Whipped
Cream Cheese

1 cup chopped fresh spinach

1 14-ounce can artichoke hearts,
drained and diced

1/4 cup roasted red peppers, diced

1 teaspoon minced garlic

1 teaspoon kosher salt

1/2 teaspoon coarsely ground
black pepper

1/4 teaspoon cayenne pepper

Preheat oven to 350°F.

In a bowl, combine olive oil, thyme, oregano, salt and pepper.

Place bagel wedges in a large mixing bowl, drizzle with the oil mixture and toss thoroughly for 60-90 seconds, or until the wedges are evenly coated.

Place the bagel wedges on a cookie sheet in a single layer and bake for 12-15 minutes, or until golden brown.

To prepare the dip, place all ingredients in a mixing bowl and stir with a rubber spatula until thoroughly blended. Makes 6-8 servings.

Skewered Chicken with California Avocado
California Avocado Commission

1 cup fresh lime juice

1/2 cup fresh cilantro leaves, chopped

2 ripe fresh California avocados, halved, seeded, peeled and cut into 3/4-inch cubes

16 10-inch wooden skewers, cut in half using heavy-duty scissors

2 chicken breasts or thighs, skinned, boned, cooked and cut into 3/4-inch cubes

1 large mango, peeled and cut into 3/4-inch cubes

1 large red bell pepper, cut into 3/4-inch squares

1 12-ounce package Mexican-style Manchego cheese, cut into 3/4-inch cubes

Lime wedges, for garnish

In a bowl, combine lime juice, cilantro and avocado cubes; set aside.

Thread each skewer alternately with cubes of avocado, chicken, mango, bell pepper and cheese.

Brush all sides of each completed skewer with remaining lime cilantro mixture.

Serve with lime wedges, so that guests can squeeze fresh lime on their skewers as they eat them. Makes 8 servings.

Tip: Large avocados are recommended for this recipe—about 8 ounces. If using smaller or larger avocados, adjust the quantity accordingly.

Provided by California Avocado Commission, Calavo Growers, Index Fresh, West Pak Avocado, Mission Produce, McDaniel Fruit, Giumarra and Del Rey Avocado.

Veggie/Bacon Parmesan Cheese Crackers
Kirkland Signature

2 pieces Kirkland Signature* Parmesan Cracker Bread

2 ounces grilled red and yellow peppers

2 ounces grilled eggplant

3 bacon strips, cooked

2 ounces mozzarella cheese, grated

Preheat oven to 450°F.

Break each piece of cracker bread in half and place on a baking sheet.

Slice peppers and eggplant into thin strips. Break bacon into 1-inch pieces.

Divide peppers and eggplant among cracker pieces. Top with bacon. Sprinkle with mozzarella.

Bake for about 3 minutes, or until cheese has melted.

Serve hot or cold. Makes 2-4 servings.

* Brands may vary by region; substitute a similar product.

Asparagus Crostini
Gourmet Trading/Jacobs Malcolm & Burtt/NewStar Fresh Foods

2 baguettes, sliced into
$1/2$-inch slices
1 cup olive oil
Sea salt and pepper
2 $1/4$ pounds asparagus
1 $1/2$ pounds
smoked salmon
1 round of imported Brie

Preheat oven to 350°F. Line a sheet pan with parchment paper.

With a pastry brush, lightly brush baguette slices with olive oil. Lay on the prepared sheet pan. Season to taste with salt and pepper. Bake for 5-7 minutes, or until golden.

To prepare the asparagus, boil in water for 2-3 minutes and then drain. Cut into 1-inch pieces.

To assemble, place a small piece of salmon on each of the crostini, then 2 pieces of asparagus. Top with 1 small slice of Brie. Garnish with fresh cracked pepper. Serve immediately. Makes 15-25 servings.

Chicken and Vegetable Bruschetta
Campbell's

1 10 $3/4$-ounce can
Campbell's Condensed
Cream of Mushroom
Soup (regular or 98%
Fat Free)
1 14 $1/2$-ounce can diced
tomatoes, drained
1 small eggplant, peeled
and diced (about
2 cups)
1 large zucchini, diced
(about 2 cups)
1 small onion, chopped
(about $1/4$ cup)
1 pound skinless, boneless
chicken breasts
$1/4$ cup shredded
Parmesan cheese, plus
more for garnish
2 tablespoons chopped
fresh parsley or basil,
plus more for garnish
Thinly sliced Italian bread,
toasted

Stir soup, tomatoes, eggplant, zucchini and onion in a 6-quart slow cooker. Add chicken and turn to coat. Cover and cook on low for 6-7 hours (or on high for 4-5 hours), or until chicken is fork-tender.

Remove chicken from the cooker to a cutting board and let stand for 5 minutes. Using 2 forks, shred the chicken. Return the chicken to the cooker.

Stir in $1/4$ cup Parmesan and 2 tablespoons parsley.

Serve on toasted bread slices. Sprinkle with additional Parmesan and chopped parsley, if desired.
Makes 7 servings.

Tip: The chicken mixture is also delicious served over hot cooked rice or pasta.

Clams Casino
Cedar Key Aquaculture Farms

1/2 cup fresh
bread crumbs

4 tablespoons butter,
softened

2 tablespoons finely
chopped red bell pepper

2 tablespoons finely
chopped fresh parsley

1 tablespoon finely
chopped green onions

1/2 teaspoon cayenne
pepper

24 Cedar Key Sweets*
farm-raised clams

6 bacon slices, cooked crisp
and crumbled

Preheat the broiler.

Combine bread crumbs, butter, bell pepper, parsley, green onions and cayenne pepper in a bowl; blend well.

Shuck clams, leaving loosened clam meat in one half of the shell; discard the other half.

Place clams on the half shell in a baking dish and cover each with about 1 teaspoon of the bread-crumb mixture.

Broil clams 4-6 inches from the heat for 3-4 minutes, or until browned.

Garnish with bacon and serve immediately. Makes 4 servings.

Brands may vary by region; substitute a similar product.

Seared Ahi Tuna Appetizer
Western United Fish Company

3/4 cup soy sauce

1/2 cup pineapple juice

1 teaspoon wasabi powder

1 tablespoon toasted
sesame oil

2 Western United Fish
Company* ahi
tuna steaks

Canola oil

Green leaf lettuce

In a small bowl, combine soy sauce, pineapple juice, wasabi and sesame oil for the marinade.

Cut ahi steaks into 2-by-2-inch portions. Place in the marinade and refrigerate for 10 minutes.

Preheat grill to high and brush with canola oil. Grill ahi for 2 minutes per side, or until seared.

Cut ahi into 1/4-inch strips and arrange on a bed of lettuce. Serve immediately. Makes 4-6 servings.

Brands may vary by region; substitute a similar product.

Your Direct Source

In The Kitchen The Costco Way

Norwegian Smoked Salmon Roll with Cream Cheese
Kirkland Signature/Foppen

9 ounces cream cheese, at room temperature

4 dill sprigs, chopped

1 teaspoon garlic powder

1 teaspoon chili powder

9 ounces Kirkland Signature* Norwegian Smoked Salmon

1 teaspoon cracked black pepper

Place cream cheese, dill, garlic powder and chili powder in a bowl and stir to blend.

Tear off 2 pieces of aluminum foil about 16 inches long.

Cut two 6-by-12-inch rectangles of smoked salmon and place one on each sheet of foil. Spread the cream cheese mixture on the salmon. Carefully roll up the salmon and then wrap in the foil. Place in the freezer for at least 2 hours.

Remove the salmon rolls from the freezer at least 1 hour before cutting.

Cut the salmon rolls in 1-inch-thick slices.

Roll the slices through the cracked black pepper. Makes 12 servings.

Brands may vary by region; substitute a similar product.

Fresh Mozzarella Appetizer with Fruit, Baby Greens and Vanilla Vinaigrette
BelGioioso

4 cups baby spring
  salad greens
1 pound BelGioioso* Fresh
  Mozzarella, sliced
2 nectarines, thinly sliced
1 pint fresh raspberries
1 pint fresh blueberries

VANILLA VINAIGRETTE
1/2 cup rice wine vinegar
4 tablespoons honey
1 cup olive oil
1/4 teaspoon salt
1/4 teaspoon freshly
  ground pepper
1 vanilla bean

Chill an appetizer platter in the refrigerator.

To prepare the vinaigrette, place vinegar, honey, olive oil, salt and pepper in a blender. Split vanilla bean and scrape seeds into the blender. Blend and set aside.

Place salad greens on the chilled platter.

Arrange mozzarella and nectarine slices on top of greens, alternating cheese and fruit.

Garnish with raspberries and blueberries.

Generously drizzle vinaigrette over the cheese and fruit. Serve immediately. Makes 8-12 servings.

Brands may vary by region; substitute a similar product.

BelGioioso®
(bel-joy-oso)

Savory and Sweet Mango Wraps
Profood

8-12 strips Philippine
  Brand* dried mango
  (or more to your liking)
1/3 cup whipped
  cream cheese
2 8-inch (burrito size)
  flour tortillas
2 green onions, green tops
  only, sliced
1/2 small red bell pepper,
  sliced into thin strips
3 ounces thinly sliced
  smoked turkey or ham

Pour boiling water over mango strips and soak for about 5-10 minutes to reconstitute. Drain and pat dry.

Spread cream cheese over tortillas and layer with mango, green onions, bell pepper and sliced meat. Roll up tightly.

Gently squeeze rolls to secure ingredients, then cut into 1/2-inch-thick slices. Makes 4-6 servings.

Brands may vary by region; substitute a similar product.

Philippine
BRAND

Dates and Peppered Grapes
Anthony Vineyards/Sun Date

1 1/2 teaspoons olive oil
4 red seedless grapes
Freshly ground black pepper
4 Medjool dates, pitted

2 ounces goat cheese
2 ounces salted pistachios, roasted and chopped

Pour olive oil onto a plate. Add grapes and roll to coat. Grind pepper onto grapes. Set aside.

Slice open dates and flatten between your hands; set aside.

Divide goat cheese into 4 pieces. Place each piece in your hand and flatten with the heel of your other hand.

To assemble, place each grape on a flattened date and set in the center of the flattened goat cheese. Form the cheese around the date-grape, covering completely. Roll in chopped pistachios. Makes 4 servings.

Turkey-Cranberry Appetizer Pizza
Pillsbury

- 2 8-ounce cans Pillsbury refrigerated crescent dinner rolls
- 8 ounces Kirkland Signature sliced smoked turkey
- 1/3 cup sweetened dried cranberries
- 6 ounces shredded fontina or Swiss cheese
- 1 tablespoon Kirkland Signature butter or margarine
- 1 garlic clove, finely chopped
- 1 teaspoon dried rosemary leaves, crushed

Preheat oven to 350°F.

Unroll 1 can of dough on a greased cookie sheet. Press into a 12-by-8-inch rectangle, pressing perforations to seal.

Top with turkey, cranberries and cheese to within 1/4 inch of edges.

Unroll remaining can of dough; press into an 11-by-8-inch rectangle, pressing perforations to seal. Cut ten 8-inch strips; place dough strips over the cheese. Tuck ends of strips under the dough.

In a small microwavable bowl, microwave butter and garlic, uncovered, on high for about 10 seconds. Brush dough with garlic butter; sprinkle with rosemary.

Bake for 25-30 minutes, or until the edges are browned and the center is set, covering with foil during the last 10 minutes if necessary to prevent excessive browning. Remove to a cooling rack for 5-10 minutes. Cut into 24 squares, then cut each square in half diagonally. Makes 48 servings.

Ginger Spiced Nuts 'n Chex Mix
General Mills

- 1/4 cup sugar
- 1/2 teaspoon ground ginger
- 1/4 teaspoon ground red pepper (cayenne)
- 1/4 cup butter or margarine
- 2 cups Corn Chex cereal
- 2 cups Rice Chex cereal
- 2 cups Wheat Chex cereal
- 2 cups Kirkland Signature extra fancy mixed nuts (from 40-ounce container)
- 1/2 cup Kirkland Signature sweetened dried cranberries
- 1/4 cup chopped crystallized ginger

In a small bowl, mix sugar, ground ginger and red pepper; set aside.

In a large microwavable bowl, microwave butter, uncovered, on high for about 40 seconds, or until melted. Stir in cereal and nuts until evenly coated. Stir in sugar mixture until evenly coated.

Microwave on high for 3-4 minutes, stirring every minute, or until the mixture just begins to brown. Stir in cranberries and crystallized ginger.

Spread on waxed paper to cool, about 15 minutes. Store in an airtight container. Makes 18 servings.

Sweet and Spicy Mixed Nuts
Ann's House of Nuts/Harvest Manor Farms

Silpat or parchment paper

4 tablespoons corn syrup

4 tablespoons sugar

1/4 teaspoon Worcestershire sauce

1/4 teaspoon cayenne pepper

1/4 teaspoon Chinese
   five-spice powder

1/8 teaspoon ground cumin

Up to 1 tablespoon freshly squeezed
   orange juice

2 cups Kirkland Signature Extra
   Fancy Mixed Nuts

Preheat oven to 350°F. Line a cookie sheet with Silpat or greased parchment paper.

In a bowl, combine corn syrup, sugar, Worcestershire sauce, cayenne, five-spice powder, cumin and enough orange juice to blend; the mixture will be thick. Add nuts, mixing gently to coat.

Spread the nuts on the prepared cookie sheet.

Bake for 5 minutes; then stir to coat. Bake 10 minutes longer, or until bubbly.

Immediately turn the nuts onto a sheet of parchment paper, as the coating hardens quickly. Keep turning and separating until the nuts no longer stick to the parchment or each other; the nuts should be cooled individually, not clumped together. Makes 6-8 servings.

Salads and Soups

Spinach, Chicken and Apple Salad
Fresh Innovations of California/
Boskovich Farms

2 tablespoons red
   wine vinegar

1 teaspoon Dijon mustard

3/4 teaspoon salt

1/4 teaspoon freshly ground
   black pepper

1/3 cup vegetable oil

1 pound (9-10 cups)
   Boskovich Farms*
   Fresh 'n' Quick spinach

1/2 pound smoked chicken
   breasts, sliced

1 6-ounce bag Prize
   Slice* organic sliced
   apples, chopped

3/4 cup chopped walnuts

1/3 pound sliced bacon,
   cooked and crumbled

1 small red onion,
   finely chopped

In a small bowl, whisk together vinegar, mustard, salt and pepper. Slowly add oil and continue to whisk until blended. Set aside.

In a large bowl, combine spinach, chicken, apples, walnuts, bacon and red onion. Add dressing just before serving and toss well. Makes 4 servings.

Tip: Use smoked turkey breast instead of chicken or sliced almonds instead of walnuts.

Brands may vary by region; substitute a similar product.

Fresh Blueberry Fennel Salad
Naturipe Farms

1 1/2 cups Naturipe
   Farms* fresh
   blueberries

1/2 cup chopped cucumber

1/2 cup diced fresh
   pineapple

1/2 cup very thinly sliced
   fresh fennel
   (1 small bulb)

2 cups cooked orzo
   pasta, cooled

1 1/2 teaspoons
   rice vinegar

1 teaspoon toasted
   sesame oil

1 teaspoon toasted
   sesame seeds

Salt and pepper to taste

Combine all ingredients in a large bowl.

Serve cold or at room temperature. Makes 6 servings.

Tips: Add 1 cup diced cooked chicken. Serve with fresh salad greens.

Brands may vary by region; substitute a similar product.

Spring Bouquet Salad
Dole

¹/₂ **pound Dole* asparagus, cut into ¹/₂-inch pieces**

8 cups Dole* Classic Iceberg Salad

1 cup halved Dole* strawberries

¹/₂ **cup bottled fat-free *or* regular raspberry vinaigrette**

¹/₃ **cup crumbled blue cheese *or* feta cheese**

¹/₄ **cup sliced almonds, toasted**

Cook asparagus in boiling water in a large saucepan for 2 minutes, or until tender-crisp. Drain and immediately plunge into ice water. Let stand for 5 minutes; drain.

Toss salad blend, strawberries and asparagus in a large bowl. Pour dressing over the salad and toss to evenly coat. Sprinkle with cheese and almonds. Makes 4 servings.

Tip: To cook asparagus in the microwave, place in a microwave-safe dish with 1 tablespoon water. Cover and microwave on high for 3-5 minutes, or until tender-crisp, stirring once during heating. Proceed as above, draining and placing asparagus in ice water.

* Brands may vary by region; substitute a similar product.

Pink Lady Apple Salad with Creamy Provolone Dressing
BelGioioso

DRESSING

¹/₂ **cup half-and-half**

¹/₂ **cup buttermilk**

1 ¹/₂ cups diced Belgioioso* Mild Provolone cheese

1 tablespoon whole-grain mustard

2 tablespoons minced shallot

1 teaspoon grated lemon peel

1 teaspoon kosher salt

1 teaspoon cracked black pepper

2 tablespoons minced fresh chives

SALAD

6 cups mixed spring greens

3 cups diced Pink Lady apples

1 cup toasted pecans

1 cup crumbled cooked bacon

To prepare the dressing, place half-and-half, buttermilk, provolone, mustard, shallots, lemon peel, salt and pepper in a blender or food processor and blend until smooth. Transfer to a small bowl. Stir in chives. Taste and adjust seasoning.

Place spring greens in a large bowl. Add dressing and toss to mix.

Divide salad among 6 plates. Top with apples, pecans and bacon. Makes 6 servings.

* Brands may vary by region; substitute a similar product.

Harvest Spring Salad with Cranberries and Walnuts
Taylor Fresh Organic

6 cups Taylor Fresh Organic* Spring Mix

½ cup chopped walnuts

½ cup dried cranberries

½ cup feta cheese

DRESSING

½ cup olive oil

3 tablespoons red wine vinegar

1 tablespoon lemon juice

2 tablespoons sugar

½ teaspoon salt

½ teaspoon dry mustard

½ tablespoon minced shallot

In a large bowl, combine spring mix, walnuts, dried cranberries and feta.

To prepare the dressing, combine all ingredients in a small bowl, stirring well with a whisk.

Pour the dressing over the salad and toss to coat. Makes 6-8 servings.

Brands may vary by region; substitute a similar product.

Curried Chicken Strawberry Salad
Naturipe Farms

1 tablespoon butter

1 tablespoon curry powder

2 tablespoons sour cream

Juice of 1 lime

1 tablespoon honey

2 cups shredded cooked chicken

⅓ cup sliced celery

1 cup cubed Naturipe Farms* strawberries

Salt and pepper

Salad greens or bread

Melt butter in a small saucepan over medium-high heat. Add curry powder and cook until fragrant, stirring constantly. Remove from the heat and stir in sour cream, lime juice and honey.

Combine chicken and celery in a bowl. Pour curry dressing over meat and stir to coat evenly. Add strawberries and stir gently to combine. Season to taste with salt and pepper.

Serve over salad greens or on fresh bread. Makes 6 servings.

Brands may vary by region; substitute a similar product.

Red Grapefruit, Feta and Mint Salad
Greene River Marketing/Tropicana

2 Tropicana* fresh
  red grapefruits

1 cucumber, halved
  lengthwise and sliced

1 medium red onion,
  thinly sliced

1 cup crumbled
  feta cheese

2 tablespoons chopped
  fresh mint

1 cup kalamata olives
  (optional)

2 tablespoons high-quality
  balsamic vinegar

Use a small sharp knife to peel grapefruit and remove the grapefruit segments. Discard the membrane.

Place grapefruit, cucumber, red onion, feta, mint and olives in a bowl and toss with balsamic vinegar.

Divide among serving plates. Makes 4 servings.

Brands may vary by region; substitute a similar product.

Grape and Orange Spinach Salad
Nature's Partner/Kings River Packing

1 6-ounce bag
  baby spinach

1/2 cup sliced almonds,
  toasted

3/4 cup Nature's Partner*
  green seedless
  grapes, halved

3/4 cup Nature's Partner*
  red seedless
  grapes, halved

2 Kings River* oranges,
  peeled and cut into
  bite-size pieces

1/2 cup feta cheese
  crumbles

Raspberry vinaigrette
  dressing

Combine spinach, almonds, grapes, oranges and feta in a large bowl, mixing well.

Spoon the salad onto individual plates and serve with raspberry vinaigrette dressing. Makes 4-6 servings.

Brands may vary by region; substitute a similar product.

Fuyu Persimmon, Kiwifruit and Prosciutto Salad
Regatta Tropicals

3 medium-sized Regatta Tropicals Fuyu persimmons

2 large Regatta Tropicals kiwifruit (peeled or unpeeled)

3 cups small arugula leaves

1 Belgian endive, leaves separated

12 thin slices prosciutto, halved lengthwise

3/4 cup walnut halves, coarsely broken

1 cup shaved Parmesan cheese

Salt and pepper

WALNUT DRESSING

2 tablespoons walnut oil

2 tablespoons extra-virgin olive oil

1 1/2 tablespoons balsamic vinegar

1 small garlic clove, crushed

1/4 cup light cream

To prepare the dressing, place walnut oil, olive oil, vinegar and garlic in a food processor/blender/mixer and process until well blended. With the motor running, add cream in a steady stream until the mixture emulsifies and is smooth. Be careful not to overmix, as the dressing may curdle.

Using a very sharp knife, cut persimmons and kiwifruit in horizontal slices; 1/16 inch works best for presentation purposes, exposing the starlike pattern of the persimmon and the vibrant color of the kiwifruit.

Arrange arugula, endive, prosciutto and walnuts in the center of the plates. Place persimmon and kiwifruit slices randomly throughout the salad.

Top with Parmesan and drizzle with dressing just before serving. Season to taste with salt and pepper. Makes 6 servings.

Mediterranean Watermelon Salad
Dulcinea

1 5-ounce bag baby romaine lettuce

3/4 cup crumbled goat cheese

2 cups cubed Dulcinea PureHeart seedless watermelon

1/4 cup extra-virgin olive oil

1/3 cup white balsamic vinegar

Sea salt and freshly ground pepper

3/4 cup walnut pieces

Toss lettuce, cheese and watermelon in a serving bowl.

Whisk oil and vinegar in a small bowl until well blended. Season to taste with salt and pepper.

Toss salad with dressing.

Top salad with walnuts and serve. Makes 6 servings.

Orange Chicken with Mixed Greens
SunWest

³/₄ cup fresh orange juice

¹/₄ cup honey

3 large garlic cloves, minced

2 tablespoons fresh thyme, minced

1 tablespoon grated orange peel

8 boneless, skinless chicken breast halves, cut in half

Salt and pepper

DRESSING

5 tablespoons olive oil

1 tablespoon toasted sesame oil

¹/₂ cup rice vinegar

2 shallots, minced

¹/₃ cup orange juice

1 garlic clove, minced

1 pound mixed salad greens

1 orange or yellow bell pepper, thinly sliced

Segments from 3 SunWest oranges (or 6 SunWest mandarins)

Fresh thyme sprigs, slivered almonds, sesame seeds and pinch of cayenne pepper, for garnish (optional)

Mix orange juice, honey, garlic, thyme and orange peel in a glass dish (or zipper-lock bag). Add chicken. Chill overnight, turning occasionally.

Season chicken with salt and pepper; grill or broil chicken until cooked through.

Pour remaining marinade into a saucepan and boil until reduced; keep warm.

To prepare the dressing, whisk together olive oil, sesame oil, vinegar, shallots, orange juice and garlic. Add salt and pepper to taste.

Combine greens, bell pepper and orange segments in a bowl; toss with the dressing. Arrange greens on a platter.

Slice the chicken, arrange on the greens and drizzle with remaining marinade. Garnish as desired. Makes 8 servings.

Cherry Chicken Salad Wraps
Grant J. Hunt Company

1 tablespoon vegetable oil

8 ounces boneless, skinless chicken, cut in thin strips

1 ¹/₂ cups pitted and halved Orchard View Farms* cherries

1 cup bean sprouts

1 cup carrots cut in thin julienne strips

1 teaspoon grated fresh ginger

³/₄ teaspoon garlic salt

¹/₈ teaspoon ground black pepper

¹/₂ cup diagonally sliced green onions

3 tablespoons soy sauce

2 tablespoons lemon juice

1 teaspoon honey

¹/₄-¹/₂ teaspoon red pepper flakes

8 large lettuce leaves such as Bibb, Boston or leafy green

Heat oil over medium-high heat in a skillet. Add chicken and sauté until lightly browned. Add cherries, bean sprouts, carrots, ginger, garlic salt and pepper. Sauté just until the bean sprouts are crisp-tender. Add green onions and sauté 1 minute longer.

In a bowl, combine soy sauce, lemon juice, honey and red pepper flakes.

To serve, place about ¹/₃ cup of the sautéed mixture in the middle of a lettuce leaf, spoon the soy sauce mixture over the sautéed mixture, and wrap the lettuce over the filling to eat out of hand like a taco. Makes 4 servings.

Tip: For a delicious sweet-tart salad, use ³/₄ cup cherries and ³/₄ cup thinly sliced Blue Goose* Italian prunes. When cherries are not available, 1 ¹/₂ cups thinly sliced Italian prunes can be substituted.

Brands may vary by region; substitute a similar product.

Spicy Cold Ginger Mango Tango Chicken Salad
Odwalla

2 tablespoons chopped fresh ginger (leave skin on)

1/2 teaspoon salt

3/4 cup Odwalla Mango Tango Fruit Smoothie Blend

1 cup Odwalla* Summertime Lime Limeade

1 garlic clove, smashed, then chopped

1 whole boneless, skinless chicken breast (or thighs)

1 head butter lettuce

3 green onions, thinly sliced on the diagonal

1 carrot, grated or thinly sliced on the diagonal

In a nonreactive bowl, stir together ginger, salt, Mango Tango, Summertime Lime and garlic. Add chicken and marinate for 20 minutes to 2 hours.

Pour off marinade into a small saucepan and simmer until it is reduced by half. Let cool.

Grill the chicken. Place in a storage container and let cool. Pour cooled marinade over cooled chicken and its juices. Refrigerate overnight.

Just before serving, remove chicken from the marinade and slice on the diagonal into thin strips.

Arrange lettuce on plates. Place chicken on lettuce, then top with green onions and carrots.

Stir the marinade and adjust seasoning to taste. Thin with water if it's too spicy. Spoon a little over each serving. Makes 4 servings.

Brands may vary by region; substitute a similar product.

Chicken Salad with Avocado
Chilean Hass Avocados

3 ounces cream cheese, softened

1/3 cup plain yogurt

1 celery stalk, finely chopped

1 tablespoon Dijon mustard

1 1/2 tablespoons finely chopped chives, green onion, dill or basil (reserve 1 teaspoon for garnish)

1/2 teaspoon salt

1/2 teaspoon grated lemon peel

1 teaspoon lemon juice

1 cup diced cooked chicken (from deli-roasted chicken)

3 Chilean Hass avocados

In a medium bowl, beat cream cheese. Add yogurt and mix until smooth. Stir in celery, mustard, chives, salt, and grated lemon peel and juice; mix until blended. Stir in chicken. Cover and chill until ready to serve.

To serve, rinse avocados. Cut in half. Gently lift out pit with a spoon. Spoon about 1/3 cup chicken salad into each avocado half. Garnish with a sprinkling of chives. Makes 6 servings.

Tip: If you wish, using a spoon, lift the avocado out of the peel before filling.

Sweet Onion and Orange Salad
Keystone

ORANGE VINAIGRETTE

- 1/2 cup orange juice, fresh if possible
- 1 tablespoon cider vinegar
- 1 teaspoon Dijon mustard
- 1 garlic clove, minced
- 3 tablespoons extra-virgin olive oil
- 1 teaspoon dried tarragon, more to taste
- Zest of 1 orange
- Salt and freshly ground pepper

- 2 Keystone Certified Sweet Onions, halved and sliced
- 1 fennel bulb, halved and sliced (stem and stalk removed)
- 1 orange, peeled and segmented
- 2 cups baby spinach
- 1/2 cup cannellini beans
- 1/2 cup red kidney beans
- 1/2 cup sweetened dried cranberries
- 3 ounces goat cheese (optional)
- Slivered almonds, for garnish

To prepare the vinaigrette, combine all ingredients and whisk to blend.

In a large bowl, combine onions, fennel, orange, spinach, beans, dried cranberries and 1/4 cup vinaigrette. Toss well and add more vinaigrette to taste.

Garnish with cheese and almonds.

Makes 6 servings.

Keystone

Caesar Salad with Red Onion, Roasted Peppers and Asparagus
Tanimura & Antle

- 2 Tanimura & Antle* Sweet Italian Red Onions, cut into 1-inch wedges
- 1 *each* red and yellow bell pepper, cut into 1-inch pieces
- 2 tablespoons Caesar vinaigrette or olive oil
- Salt and freshly ground black pepper
- 1 pound asparagus, cut into 2-inch lengths
- 2 Tanimura & Antle* Romaine Hearts
- 1/3 cup Caesar vinaigrette
- 1/3 cup shaved Parmesan cheese

Preheat oven to 400°F.

Toss onions and peppers with 2 tablespoons vinaigrette in a jelly roll pan to coat; spread in a single layer. Sprinkle with salt and pepper to taste. Roast for 10 minutes. Add asparagus; toss. Roast until vegetables are tender, 8-10 minutes longer. Let cool.

Separate lettuce leaves; rinse and drain well. Line a platter with some of the lettuce leaves.

Tear remaining lettuce into bite-size pieces. Combine with roasted vegetables in a bowl. Add 1/3 cup vinaigrette and toss to coat. Transfer to the platter.

Top with Parmesan and freshly ground pepper. Makes 6 servings.

Tip: The roasted vegetables can be made ahead. Let vegetables cool for 20 minutes, then refrigerate, covered. To serve this salad as a main dish, top with sliced grilled chicken or steak.

* Brands may vary by region; substitute a similar product.

Chinese Noodle and Vegetable Salad
Foxy Foods/Monterey Mushrooms

DRESSING
1/4 cup olive or vegetable oil

1/4 cup white wine vinegar

1 tablespoon toasted sesame oil

1 tablespoon soy sauce

1 tablespoon lemon juice

1 tablespoon ketchup

3/4 teaspoon salt

1/4 teaspoon grated fresh ginger

1/4 teaspoon granulated sugar

1/4 teaspoon ground pepper

SALAD
1 head Foxy* iceberg lettuce, shredded

1 bunch broccoli, cut into florets

3/4 cup sliced large white Monterey* mushrooms

1/4 cup bias-sliced celery

1/4 cup shredded carrot

1/4 cup chopped red or green bell pepper

1 cup crisp chow mein noodles

To prepare the dressing, combine all ingredients in a food processor or blender. Cover and process until well blended. Set aside.

In a large bowl, toss together lettuce, broccoli florets, mushrooms, celery, carrot and bell pepper. Drizzle dressing over the salad and toss well to coat.

Spoon the salad onto 4 plates; sprinkle with chow mein noodles. Makes 4 servings.

Brands may vary by region; substitute a similar product.

Festive Asian-Style Chicken Salad with Edamame
Okami

1 Okami* Asian-Style
  Chicken Salad Kit
  (use only 1 of each
  component)
1 cup shelled
  Okami* edamame
1 whole carrot, diced
1 11-ounce can mandarin
  oranges, drained
1/2 head iceberg
  lettuce, chopped
Fresh cilantro sprigs,
  for garnish

Combine all ingredients except cilantro in a bowl and toss with the dressing included in the kit.

Garnish with cilantro sprigs and serve. Makes 6 servings.

Brands may vary by region; substitute a similar product.

The "Anytime" Meal

Grape Tomato and Avocado Salad with Hearts of Palm
NatureSweet

1 14- to 16-ounce can
  or jar of hearts of
  palm, drained
  and sliced
1/2 cup fresh lime juice
1 cup olive oil
2 tablespoons minced
  fresh oregano
2 tablespoons minced
  fresh cilantro
Salt and pepper
60 NatureSweet*
  grape tomatoes
3 whole avocados, pitted
  and sliced
2 10-ounce bags
  fresh salad greens
  (Italian blend)
12 sprigs fresh parsley,
  for garnish

Place hearts of palm in a bowl and add lime juice, olive oil, oregano, cilantro, and salt and pepper to taste. Stir to combine. Let stand for 15 minutes. Drain; reserve liquid.

Add tomatoes and avocados to the marinated hearts of palm. Add more salt to taste.

Divide salad greens among 6 plates. Top greens with hearts of palm mixture. Drizzle 1/4 cup of reserved liquid over each salad. Garnish with parsley. Makes 6 servings.

Brands may vary by region; substitute a similar product.

California Avocado Caprese Salad
California Avocado Commission

1 ripe fresh California avocado, halved, seeded, peeled and cut into thin wedges

2 lemons, juiced

2 ripe tomatoes, cut into ¼-inch slices

8 medium fresh basil leaves

1 8-ounce ball fresh mozzarella cheese, cut into ¼-inch slices

¼ cup lemon-scented olive oil

3 tablespoons capers, drained

Sea salt

Freshly ground black pepper

Place avocado slices in a shallow bowl and dress with lemon juice, making sure all slices are coated.

On individual salad plates, layer tomato slice, fresh basil leaf, mozzarella slice and avocado slice. Repeat with a second tomato slice, fresh basil leaf, mozzarella slice and avocado slice alongside. Drizzle with lemon-scented olive oil and sprinkle capers over all. Repeat the process for each plate.

Season with sea salt and freshly ground black pepper to taste. Makes 4 servings.

Tip: Large avocados are recommended for this recipe—about 8 ounces. If using smaller or larger avocados, adjust the quantity accordingly.

Provided by California Avocado Commission, Calavo Growers, Index Fresh, West Pak Avocado, Mission Produce, McDaniel Fruit, Giumarra and Del Rey Avocado.

Southwestern Seven-Layer Salad with Corn Muffin Croutons
Best Brands Corp.

3 Kirkland Signature corn muffins, cut into 1-inch chunks
1/2 cup real mayonnaise
1 tablespoon white wine vinegar
1/2 teaspoon chili powder
1/2 teaspoon paprika
1/4 teaspoon garlic powder
1/4 teaspoon cayenne pepper
2 dashes Tabasco sauce
6-8 cups romaine lettuce (1 large or 2 small heads), washed, torn into pieces, spun dry
1/2 cup black beans, rinsed, drained
1/2 cup frozen corn kernels
1/2 red bell pepper, cut into thin strips
1 cup cherry tomatoes, halved
1/2 medium red onion, thinly sliced

Preheat oven to 400°F. Place muffin chunks on a baking pan. Toast in the oven until golden brown, turning once to prevent burning, about 5-10 minutes. Let cool. (Do not prepare more than 2 hours ahead.)

In a small bowl, whisk together mayonnaise, vinegar and seasonings. Refrigerate until ready to use.

Toss lettuce with the dressing in a large bowl. Place dressed lettuce on a large serving platter or on individual plates.

Top lettuce with each of the remaining ingredients, in order.

Top with corn muffin croutons.

Serve immediately. Makes 6-8 servings.

Best Brands Corp.

Summer Orange and Date Salad with Mint
Outspan Oranges/
Bard Valley Medjool Date Growers

6 Outspan* oranges
6 Medjool dates, chopped
1/2 cup slivered almonds
2 tablespoons chopped fresh mint
2 tablespoons fresh lemon juice
1 teaspoon superfine sugar
Mint sprigs, for garnish (optional)

Peel oranges, removing all white pith, and slice crosswise into "cartwheels." Place in a glass salad bowl.

Garnish with dates, almonds and mint.

Sprinkle with lemon juice and sugar. Chill.

To serve, garnish with mint sprigs, if desired. Makes 6 servings.

* Brands may vary by region; substitute a similar product.

FISHER CAPESPAN

OUTSPAN®

Medjool Dates

Veggie Mix Pasta Salad in Parmesan Crisps
Kirkland Signature/NutriVerde

4 cups Normandy Blend frozen vegetable mix

1 cup dried fusilli or other short pasta

1 cup grated Parmesan cheese

1 tablespoon flour

¼ cup balsamic vinegar

1 teaspoon sugar (optional)

½ cup olive oil

1 tablespoon chopped fresh herbs (basil, thyme)

Salt and pepper

18 large capers, for garnish

Steam vegetable mix to thaw and place in a bowl.

Cook pasta in boiling salted water until al dente. Drain and add to the vegetables.

Preheat oven to 350°F.

Mix cheese and flour. Shape into 6 (5-inch) circles on a nonstick baking tray. Bake for about 5-7 minutes, or until browned. Remove from the oven. Lift the circles carefully with a spatula and place over small bowls or muffin tins to shape.

In a small bowl, mix vinegar, sugar, olive oil, herbs, and salt and pepper to taste. Add to the pasta and vegetables; toss until well mixed.

Fill the cheese crisps with salad and garnish with capers. Makes 6 servings.

Clementine, Avocado, Celery and Radish Salad with Balsamic Syrup
Duda Farm Fresh Foods, Inc.

4 Dandy* clementines

1 avocado

2 stalks Dandy* celery

2 Dandy* radishes

2-3 tablespoons
    balsamic syrup

1/4 teaspoon kosher salt

Freshly ground
    black pepper

Peel clementines and divide into segments.

Peel and dice avocado.

Cut celery into 2-inch-long julienne strips or slice crosswise.

Cut radishes into julienne strips.

Place fruit and vegetables in a bowl and toss with balsamic syrup, salt and pepper to taste. Serve chilled. Makes 4 servings.

Tip: If you cannot find prepared balsamic syrup, you can make it by reducing 2 cups balsamic vinegar to about 1/3 cup over medium-high heat in a stainless-steel or enamel saucepan, being careful not to burn it.

Brands may vary by region; substitute a similar product.

Golden Citrus Salad
Noble Worldwide/ Diversified Citrus Marketing

1/2 cup sugar

2 envelopes unflavored
    gelatin

1 cup chilled Florida
    orange juice

1 cup apricot nectar

3 cups assorted chopped
    and seeded Florida
    citrus sections
    (oranges, tangerines
    or grapefruit)

DRESSING

4 ounces reduced-
    fat cream cheese
    (Neufchatel), softened

1 tablespoon sugar

1 teaspoon finely shredded
    Florida orange peel

3-4 tablespoons Florida
    orange juice

In a medium saucepan, combine sugar and gelatin; stir in 2 cups cold water. Cook and stir over medium heat until sugar and gelatin dissolve.

Remove from the heat. Stir in orange juice and apricot nectar. Transfer to a bowl. Chill until the mixture is partially set.

Fold in citrus sections. Pour into a 6-cup mold. Cover and chill until set. Unmold to serve.

To prepare the dressing, stir together cream cheese, sugar, orange peel and enough of the orange juice for desired consistency.

Drizzle dressing over the salad. Makes 8-10 servings.

Sweet Italian Sausage and Vegetable Soup
Premio

1/2 cup olive oil

3 tablespoons butter

5 links Premio* sweet Italian sausage, removed from casings and crumbled

1 cup thinly sliced onions

1 cup diced carrots

1 cup diced celery

2 cups peeled, diced potatoes

2 cups diced zucchini

1 cup diced green beans

3 cups shredded Savoy (curly) cabbage

6-8 cups meat or chicken broth, fresh or canned

1 cup canned diced Italian tomatoes with juice

2-3 cups water

1 1/2 cups canned cannellini beans, drained

Salt and pepper

1 cup white rice

Pesto or grated Parmesan cheese

Heat olive oil and butter in a large soup or stock pot. Add sausage meat and sauté over high heat just to brown.

Add fresh vegetables in the order listed, cooking over high heat for 3-4 minutes after each addition. After adding cabbage, cook for 8-10 minutes.

Add broth, tomatoes and water. Bring to a simmer and add beans. Simmer, uncovered, for 2 hours. Season to taste with salt and pepper.

Add rice, cover and simmer for 30 minutes.

Check seasoning and serve with pesto or grated Parmesan. Makes 6 servings.

Tip: Use hot Italian sausage for a spicier flavor.

* Brands may vary by region; substitute a similar product.

Bacon and Caramelized Onion Chowder
Kirkland Signature/Darigold/ Michael Cutler Company

3 tablespoons Kirkland Signature butter, divided

2 tablespoons olive oil

One jumbo-size sweet onion, peeled and vertically sliced (about 3 cups)

1/2 cup shredded carrots

1 package (1 lb. 4 oz.) partially cooked red potato wedges, cut in half (such as Simply Potatoes Red Potato Wedges)

3/4 cup precooked bacon bits (such as Hormel Real Crumbled Bacon), plus more for garnish

2 ounces cream cheese, cubed

3 cups Kirkland Signature whole milk

Darigold* sour cream

Chopped fresh parsley

Shredded Cheddar cheese

Set a 3-quart stock pot over medium-high heat for 30 seconds. Add 2 tablespoons butter and olive oil; stir in onions and sauté until lightly browned and caramelized (about 10-15 minutes). Remove onions and set aside.

Add carrots and 1 tablespoon butter to the pot; sauté until carrots are tender, about 2 minutes. Add potato wedges and sauté for 3 minutes, or until potatoes are slightly browned. Stir in onions and 3/4 cup bacon bits.

Reduce heat to medium; add cream cheese and stir until melted. Add milk and cook, gently stirring, until the soup begins to thicken.

Serve with a dollop of sour cream, crumbled bacon, parsley and a sprinkling of Cheddar cheese. Makes 6-8 servings.

Tips: Cooked bacon strips, diced, can be substituted. Partially cooked diced potatoes with onions can be substituted.

Brands may vary by region; substitute a similar product.

Santa Fe Chicken and Potato Soup
Top Brass/Farm Fresh Direct

2 medium russet, white or yellow potatoes, or 3-4 small red potatoes

1 boneless chicken breast (6-8 ounces)

1 14 1/2-ounce can diced tomatoes and chiles

1 14-ounce can chicken broth

1 1 1/4-ounce packet taco seasoning

Cut potatoes into 1/2-inch cubes.

On a separate cutting board, cut chicken into uniform cubes.

In a 1-quart microwave-safe dish, combine potatoes, chicken, tomatoes, broth and taco seasoning, mixing well. Cover tightly with a lid or plastic wrap.

Microwave on high for 15 minutes (cooking time may vary depending on your microwave), or until potatoes and chicken are done. Let sit for 2 minutes. Use oven mitts or tongs to remove the dish from the microwave. Remove plastic wrap carefully to prevent burns from steam. Makes 4 servings.

Courtesy of the U.S. Potato Board.

Asian Chicken Vegetable Rice Soup
Kirkland Signature/Gourmet Dining

16 ounces chicken breast meat, cut in ³/₄-inch cubes

2 14 ½-ounce cans chicken broth

2 tablespoons soy sauce

1 teaspoon toasted sesame oil (optional)

1 teaspoon grated fresh ginger

3 garlic cloves, minced

3 cups Kirkland Signature Vegetable Stir-Fry (frozen)

1 cup instant rice

Place chicken in a 3 ½- or 4-quart slow cooker. Combine chicken broth, soy sauce, sesame oil, ginger and garlic. Pour over the chicken.

Cover and cook on low-heat setting for 8-10 hours or on high-heat setting for 4-5 hours. Add vegetables 30 minutes before finishing.

Stir in instant rice. Cover and cook for 5-8 minutes, or until the rice is tender. Makes 6 servings.

Tips: Reduced-sodium soy sauce can be used. For variety, substitute seafood for the chicken, or cooked brown rice for the white rice.

Side Dishes

California Couscous
Stevco/Richard Bagdasarian

1 1/2 cups chicken broth
1/8- 1/4 teaspoon ground pepper
1 cup uncooked couscous
2 tablespoons lemon juice
1 1/2 cups California seedless grapes
1/4 cup chopped fresh parsley
1 tablespoon finely chopped green onions
2 tablespoons pine nuts

Bring broth and pepper to a boil in a small saucepan.

Add couscous and lemon juice; mix well. Cover, remove from the heat and let stand for 5 minutes.

Add remaining ingredients and toss lightly to mix. Serve warm. Makes 4 servings.

Recipe courtesy of the California Table Grape Commission.

Risotto with Sweet Italian Sausage and Radicchio
Premio

2 tablespoons olive oil
5 links Premio* sweet Italian sausage, removed from casings
1 medium onion, chopped fine
2 heads radicchio, cored and chopped
1 1/2 cups Arborio rice (Italian short grain)
1/2 cup dry white wine
6-8 cups chicken or vegetable broth, warmed
2 tablespoons butter
2/3 cup grated Parmesan cheese

Heat olive oil in a large heavy skillet or sauce pot over medium heat. Add sausage and onion and cook for 6-8 minutes, breaking up sausage. Add radicchio and cook for 3 minutes.

Add rice and stir until rice is hot, 3-5 minutes. Add wine and stir until dry.

Add 2 cups broth and cook, stirring often, until rice absorbs liquid. Add remaining broth 1/2 cup at a time, stirring often, until rice is creamy but still slightly al dente, 15-20 minutes.

Remove from the heat and cover for 5-8 minutes. Stir in butter and Parmesan vigorously. Serve immediately. Makes 6 servings.

* Brands may vary by region; substitute a similar product.

Four-Herb Parisian Carrot Salad
Grimmway Farms

1 pound Grimmway*
  baby carrots

2 tablespoons olive oil

1/4 cup chopped fresh dill

1/4 cup chopped
  fresh oregano

1 tablespoon chopped
  fresh thyme

1 teaspoon dried tarragon

1 teaspoon grated
  lemon peel

3 tablespoons lemon juice

1 tablespoon sugar

1 head romaine lettuce

Drop carrots into a saucepan of boiling water. Return to a boil and cook for 5 minutes, or until tender-crisp. Drain, running cold water over carrots.

Combine carrots with all other ingredients except lettuce and toss well for 2 minutes to bruise herbs and bring out flavor. Cover and chill until ready to serve.

Line a salad bowl or individual plates with lettuce. Place carrots on top. Makes 4 servings.

Brands may vary by region; substitute a similar product.

Orange Honey Teriyaki Vegetable Brochettes
Kirkland Signature/NutriVerde

4 cups Normandy Blend
  frozen vegetable mix

Bamboo skewers

3/4 cup soy sauce

1/4 cup honey

1/2 cup orange juice

1 teaspoon grated
  orange peel

1 tablespoon grated
  fresh ginger

1 teaspoon red
  pepper flakes

Slightly thaw frozen vegetables, then insert onto skewers; let thaw at room temperature.

Combine remaining ingredients in a saucepan and boil until slightly thickened.

Steam, grill or sauté the vegetable skewers. Serve with the sauce. Makes 6 servings.

Sunset Campari Risotto with Seared Scallops

Mastronardi Produce/Sunset

TOMATO JAM

15 Sunset Campari tomatoes
7 shallots, finely diced
2 garlic cloves, thinly sliced
1/2 cup extra-virgin olive oil
6 basil stems, tied together

RISOTTO

3 cups chicken stock
2 tablespoons butter
3 shallots, finely diced
1 cup Arborio rice
1 cup white wine
Salt and pepper
1/4 cup mascarpone cheese
1/3 cup grated Parmesan cheese
6 Sunset Campari tomatoes, chopped
1 tablespoon chopped fresh basil
1 tablespoon chopped fresh parsley
6 good-sized bay scallops (optional)
3 tablespoons canola oil (optional)
Lemon juice (optional)

To prepare the jam, slice an X on the top of each tomato and cut out the stem end. Drop tomatoes in boiling water for 1 minute. Remove and chill in a bowl of ice water. Peel and halve, squeezing out the seeds; roughly chop.

In a shallow pot, sauté shallots and garlic in olive oil over medium-low heat until they start to soften. Stir in tomatoes and basil stems. Cook at low simmer until thick and jamlike. Remove from the heat.

To prepare the risotto, warm stock over medium heat; keep warm.

In another pot, melt butter over medium to medium-high heat. Stir in shallots and rice; cook for 1 minute. Pour in wine and cook, stirring, until absorbed. Ladle in warm stock to cover and stir. Adjust heat so the rice is cooking at a low simmer. When stock is absorbed, ladle in more and continue stirring. Repeat the process until the rice is loose and creamy, about 20 minutes in total; remove from the heat.

Season to taste with salt and pepper. Remove basil stems, then stir in tomato jam, mascarpone, Parmesan, chopped tomatoes and herbs.

Season scallops with salt and pepper to taste. Heat canola oil in a sauté pan over medium-high heat. Add scallops and sear. Reduce the heat to medium and cook to taste. Squeeze a little lemon juice over the scallops and serve on top of the risotto. Makes 6 servings.

SUNSET
Goodness Grown Naturally

Creamed Spinach
River Ranch Fresh Foods

2 bacon slices
1 cup chicken broth
1 tablespoon butter
1 garlic clove, minced
1 teaspoon salt
$1/8$ teaspoon pepper
20 ounces River Ranch spinach (half of 40-ounce bag)
1 tablespoon flour
$1/2$ cup milk
1 teaspoon lemon juice
Lemon slices dusted with paprika, for garnish (optional)

Fry bacon in a skillet.

Remove bacon and add chicken broth, butter, garlic, salt, pepper and spinach to the pan. Cook, covered, over medium heat until tender, about 5 minutes, stirring occasionally. Drain liquid.

Place flour in a small bowl. Slowly add milk and lemon juice, stirring until smooth. Pour over the spinach. Cook over low heat until the sauce is smooth and thickened, tossing spinach with a fork.

Crumble cooked bacon and blend into the creamed spinach.

Garnish with lemon slices. Makes 4 servings.

Tip: To serve as an entrée, toss creamed spinach with your favorite cooked pasta.

Vanilla, Honey and Rosemary Pickled Sunset Splendido Tomatoes
Mastronardi Produce/Sunset

1 pint Sunset Splendido tomatoes
2 tablespoons green cardamom pods, slightly crushed
$3/8$ cup honey
$3/8$ cup white balsamic vinegar
1 cup water
$1/2$ vanilla bean, split
1 small garlic clove, sliced
1 sprig of rosemary

Bring a large pot of water to a boil. Fill a large bowl with iced water.

Carefully place tomatoes in the boiling water and boil for 30 seconds. Pour into a colander and place in iced water for 1 minute. With a small paring knife, peel the skins from the tomatoes. Place peeled tomatoes in a nonreactive bowl or container and set aside.

In a small sauté pan, toast cardamom pods over medium heat. Set aside.

In a small saucepan, bring honey to a boil. Pour in vinegar and water, and return to a boil. Reduce the heat to a simmer. Scrape out the seeds from the vanilla bean, and add the seeds and the pod to the pan. Add cardamom and garlic. Simmer for 3 minutes, skimming the foam off the top with a small ladle or spoon and discarding. Remove from the heat and add rosemary sprig. Let steep for 15 minutes.

Remove rosemary from the honey mixture and pour over the tomatoes. Cover and refrigerate for 24 hours. Makes 4-6 servings.

Goodness Grown Naturally™

Vegetable Stir-Fry
Kirkland Signature/Gourmet Dining

1/4 cup cornstarch
2 tablespoons water
1 teaspoon minced fresh ginger
1 teaspoon minced fresh garlic
1/3 cup sugar
1/4 cup soy sauce

2 tablespoons white vinegar
2 tablespoons dry sherry
1 cup chicken broth
2 1/2 tablespoons olive oil
3 cups Kirkland Signature Vegetable Stir-Fry (frozen)

Combine cornstarch, water, ginger, garlic, sugar, soy sauce, vinegar, sherry and chicken broth in a bowl. Stir or place in a closed container and shake.

Heat a large skillet or wok over medium heat. Add olive oil and vegetables and cook for 4-5 minutes, or until tender.

Add the sauce and cook until thickened. Serve over rice or noodles, if desired. Makes 2-3 servings.

Tip: Lite soy sauce, low-sodium chicken broth and sugar substitute can be used. Add grated orange peel, pineapple juice or orange juice to boost flavor.

Dana's Red Potato Salad
Skagit Valley's Best Produce/ Wallace Farms/Valley Pride

- 12 medium Washington* red potatoes
- 10 eggs, hard-boiled, peeled and sliced
- 1 small kosher dill pickle, chopped
- 1/2 medium Walla Walla sweet onion, finely chopped
- 4 celery stalks, finely chopped
- 2 cups mayonnaise
- 1 tablespoon chopped fresh dill or 1/2 teaspoon dried
- 1/2 teaspoon yellow or Dijon mustard
- Salt and pepper to taste

Preheat oven to 350°F.

Scrub potatoes with a vegetable brush under cold running water. Cut a slit in each potato, place on a cookie sheet and bake until just tender, about 30-40 minutes, depending on the size of the potatoes. Let cool, then refrigerate for 2 hours or overnight.

Reserve 1 potato and mash with hands. Cut remaining potatoes into bite-size chunks. Put all potatoes in a large bowl.

Add all remaining ingredients and mix well. Chill until ready to serve. Makes 8-10 servings.

Tip: For variety, add finely chopped green bell pepper, roasted sweet red pepper, cooked and crumbled bacon, and/or Italian dressing. Serve with parsley and pickled beets.

From Dana's Restaurant, Moses Lake, Washington.
* Brands may vary by region; substitute a similar product.

Artichoke Jalapeño Potato Pancakes
Reser's Fine Foods

- 2 1/2 cups Reser's* Mashed Potatoes
- 1/2 cup Stonemill Kitchens* Artichoke Jalapeño Dip
- 1/4 cup (2 ounces) grated Parmesan cheese
- 2 tablespoons chopped red bell pepper
- 2 tablespoons chopped fresh parsley
- 1 cup plain dry bread crumbs or panko
- Oil or clarified butter for frying

In a medium bowl, mix mashed potatoes, dip, Parmesan, bell pepper and parsley together until blended. Shape into 12 round patties, about 1 inch thick. Coat in bread crumbs and set on waxed paper.

Heat a heavy skillet on medium-low, and add oil or butter. When oil is hot, add cakes and cook until golden, about 5 minutes per side. Makes 12 cakes.

Tip: Serve as an alternative to mashed potatoes, or as an appetizer.

* Brands may vary by region; substitute a similar product.

Potato-Crusted Mushroom "Galettes"
Alsum Produce/Anthony Farms/Russet Potato Exchange

1 ounce dried porcini mushrooms

4 teaspoons olive oil

1 1/2 pounds fresh wild and domestic mushrooms, cleaned and quartered

1/4 cup diced shallots

2 teaspoons chopped garlic

2 teaspoons flour

Salt, white pepper and nutmeg

3 pounds Wisconsin* russet potatoes

1/3 cup vegetable oil

Chopped chives

Preheat oven to 400°F.

Soak porcini in 1 1/3 cups very hot water until softened. Strain, reserving liquid. Strain liquid; rinse porcini and cut in 1/2-inch pieces.

Heat olive oil in large sauté pan; add fresh mushrooms, shallots and garlic. Sauté until mushrooms start to soften; stir in flour. Add porcini and soaking liquid; simmer until sauce just coats mushrooms. Season with salt, pepper and nutmeg. Let cool.

Cut potatoes in thin lengthwise slices. Blanch in boiling water just until flexible; drain. Lay slices on a towel.

Brush 8 4 1/2-inch nonstick tartlet molds with removable bottoms with vegetable oil. Line bottoms of molds with 1 layer of potatoes. Arrange overlapping potato slices in molds, letting them hang over the sides. Brush with oil.

Place 1/2 cup mushroom mixture in each mold; fold over potato slices to cover. Brush with oil, place on a sheet pan and bake for 45 minutes, or until edges are golden. Cool slightly, unmold and sprinkle with chives. Makes 8 servings.

Brands may vary by region; substitute a similar product.

Bacon and Green Bean Casserole Deluxe
Kirkland Signature/Hormel

2 16-ounce cans green beans, drained

1 10 3/4-ounce can condensed cream of mushroom soup

3/4 cup milk

1 2.8-ounce can French fried onions, divided

3 ounces Hormel* Real Crumbled Bacon or Hormel/Kirkland Signature Precooked Bacon, chopped and divided

1/8 teaspoon pepper

Preheat oven to 350°F.

In a medium bowl, stir together beans, soup, milk, half of the onions, half of the bacon topping and pepper. Spoon into a 1 1/2-quart casserole.

Bake for 30 minutes. Top with remaining onions and bacon. Bake 5 minutes longer. Makes 6 servings.

Brands may vary by region; substitute a similar product.

Corn Muffins with Gourmet Butters
Best Brands Corp.

Match Kirkland Signature corn muffins to the tastes of your meals with flavored butters.

SOUTHWESTERN BUTTER

1/2 cup (1 stick) butter or margarine, softened to room temperature or spreadable consistency

2 teaspoons chili powder
3/4 teaspoon ground cumin
1/2 teaspoon cayenne pepper
2 drops Tabasco sauce

Combine all ingredients with a fork until well blended. Serve with warmed corn muffins and chili or ribs. Makes 8 servings.

CRANBERRY ORANGE BUTTER

1/2 cup (1 stick) butter or margarine, softened to room temperature or spreadable consistency

2 tablespoons frozen orange juice concentrate
1/4 cup finely chopped sweetened dried cranberries

Combine all ingredients, blending well with a fork. Serve with warmed corn muffins at Thanksgiving. Makes 8 servings.

MAPLE BUTTER

1/2 cup (1 stick) butter or margarine, softened to room temperature or spreadable consistency

2 tablespoons pure maple syrup

Combine butter and syrup, mashing together with a fork until well blended. Serve with warmed corn muffins for breakfast or anytime. Makes 8 servings.

Best Brands Corp.

Scalloped Potatoes
Tillamook

2 tablespoons Tillamook* butter, softened and divided

1 cup (4 ounces) shredded Tillamook* Vintage White Extra Sharp Cheddar Cheese

1 cup (4 ounces) shredded Tillamook* Sharp Cheddar Cheese

3 cups half-and-half

1 teaspoon salt

1/4 teaspoon freshly ground pepper

2 1/2 pounds russet potatoes (about 4 medium)

Preheat oven to 350°F.

Butter a 13-by-9-inch baking dish with 1 tablespoon butter. In a small bowl, combine cheeses; set aside.

In a 4-quart saucepan, combine half-and-half, salt and pepper.

Peel potatoes and slice 1/16 inch thick. Add to the saucepan and bring just to a simmer. Carefully pour the potato mixture into the prepared baking dish. Distribute potatoes evenly in the pan and sprinkle with cheese. Dot the top with small pieces of the remaining butter.

Bake for 45 minutes, or until the potatoes are done and the top is golden. Let rest for 10-15 minutes before serving. Makes 8 servings.

Brands may vary by region; substitute a similar product.

Tillamook®

Corn Muffin and Sausage Dressing
Best Brands Corp.

3 Kirkland Signature
   corn muffins, broken into pieces
1 6-ounce can refrigerated biscuit
   dough, baked according to
   instructions, cooled and
   broken into pieces
1/2 teaspoon celery salt
1 teaspoon poultry seasoning
1 teaspoon baking powder
Salt and pepper

2 tablespoons butter
1 cup chopped onions
1 cup thinly sliced celery
1/2 cup sliced mushrooms
1/2 cup chopped green
   bell pepper
1/2 pound seasoned pork sausage,
   browned and drained
1 egg, beaten
1 14 1/2-ounce can chicken broth

Preheat oven to 350°F. Lightly grease a 13-by-9-inch pan.

Place corn muffin and biscuit pieces in a large bowl. Add celery salt, poultry seasoning, baking powder, and salt and pepper to taste. Set aside.

Melt butter over medium heat in a sauté pan, add vegetables and cook until softened.

Gently stir cooled pork sausage and sautéed vegetables into the muffins/biscuits.

In a small bowl, combine beaten egg and chicken broth. Add to the dressing mixture and stir just until all ingredients are moistened.

Place mixture in the prepared pan. Bake for 40-45 minutes, or until set and lightly browned. Serve warm. Makes 12 servings.

Best Brands Corp.

Chef's Choice

The world's best chefs have the special ability to infuse dishes with their unique personalities. We asked several top chefs to do their magic with the products supplied by these great companies:

90

115

109

Error

103

Kitchen basics

By Martha Stewart

The recipe for success in the kitchen calls for the best ingredients, the skilled hands of the chef, equal pinches of passion and patience—and the right tools. A properly stocked pantry is also a must. Here are some essentials in terms of tools and staples to have on hand in your kitchen to help you in your culinary pursuits.

Top ten kitchen tools

Plane zester

The tiny, razor-sharp teeth of a plane zester make it the perfect tool for grating citrus fruit. When you zest a citrus fruit—that is, grate the outer layer, or colored part, of its skin—its aromatic oils are released. These oils give the zest its intense flavor. A plane zester is easy to use, requiring almost no pressure. To release the bits of zest that get caught in the holes, tap the zester on the counter. And a zester can do a lot more than zest fruit: Use it for grating hard cheeses, such as Parmesan, Pecorino and Romano, or for grating nutmeg, chocolate and ginger.

Measuring cups and spoons

These are basics that each person needs, no matter how little cooking you do: a glass measuring cup for liquid (or a few—they come sized for one to four cups); when using, read at eye level. You should also have nesting sets of spoons and cups for dry measures. As with other tools, I find that stainless steel is the best material because it is long-lasting and can be easily washed.

Wooden spoons

Be sure to have two round wooden spoons with long handles so you can stir all the way to the bottom of deep pans. One should be for savory and one for sweet, to keep each food flavor clean. Though they come in many sizes and shapes, you really need just two; you might also buy two flat wooden spoons with angled bottoms for cooked custards and other thick sauces (to get at a pan's edges).

Whisks

Handheld whisks are designed to blend ingredients without lumping and to incorporate air into liquids. They are ideal for making dressings, blending sauces, beating eggs and whipping heavy cream. They're also good for whisking together dry ingredients when baking. You can even use them to break up ground meat during cooking. Whisks should be sturdy, durable, and feel comfortable in your hand. Choose a whisk with the most wires (it'll work fastest), and make sure the wires are embedded securely in the handle. Most whisks are made of rustproof stainless steel; those with nylon-coated wires are safe to use on nonstick surfaces. Longer whisks can reach into pots and pans; shorter whisks are useful for mixing in bowls.

Tongs

Designed like giant tweezers, tongs can be used to hold and lift all kinds of food, hot or cold; they can also reach high-heat places, especially on the grill or in the oven. Tongs are ideal for turning meat as it cooks, removing baked potatoes from the oven, lifting lobsters and ears of corn out of hot water, or tossing and serving salads and pasta. Buy two pairs of tongs, one that's medium in length and the other that's long. Look for professional-grade ones (which are heavy duty and don't bend) with scalloped edges and rounded tips.

Oven thermometer

Having an oven thermometer is critical to successful cooking, especially baking—oven thermostats can be off enough to affect results dramatically. Place it in the oven to make sure that what you set the dial at is what you get; if not, adjust the temperature or cooking time accordingly. Mercury thermometers, which fold flat, are a compact alternative to the clip-on variety.

Sieve

A sieve is useful for draining liquids away from solids. It's also wonderful to have on hand when cooking with hot oil—foods that sputter and spatter as they fry, such as bacon and soft-shell crabs, can be a hazard to the cook and anyone else within close range. If you don't have a spatter guard, a large sieve can stand in for protection—just place it facedown over the food cooking in the pan. For safety, turn both handles toward the back of the stove, resting the sieve's handle on top of the pan's.

Peeler

Peelers are an essential part of any cook's collection. The ultra-sharp blade of a harp-shaped peeler is ideal for thick-skinned produce such as butternut squash, while a traditional vegetable peeler is still the best choice for thin-skinned vegetables like potatoes.

Rubber spatulas

Rubber spatulas are indispensable tools for cooking and baking. They're perfect for scraping dough and batter down the sides of bowls, and are safe to use with nonstick surfaces. It is only necessary to have two sizes: a large one and a small one (to work in narrow spaces), both with long handles.

Stainless-steel spatulas

You need a few of these inexpensive utensils: Choose at least one thin, flexible spatula in stainless steel, and one or two long, wide heavy-duty models. Use the flexible one for turning pancakes and removing cookies from cookie sheets. Long, wide ones will prove to be ideal for lifting fish out of a pan and moving it to a serving dish, or for transferring a decorated cake onto a cake stand.

Basic bakeware

Every cook needs basic bakeware, such as pie dishes, tart and muffin tins, and baking and cake pans. Here are my recommendations:

Two 9-by-13-inch baking pans
8- or 9-inch square baking pan
Half-sheet pan and/or jelly-roll pan
Two cookie sheets
Two 9-inch round cake pans
Springform pan
Angel food cake pan
Loaf pan
Bundt cake pan
Pie dish
Muffin tin

What should I keep in my pantry and for how long?

With plenty of ingredients on hand, you are always prepared, whether you're cooking for a dinner party or whipping up snacks for unexpected guests. The items you stock will depend on your culinary habits and the size of your household, but here are some guidelines.

Pantry item	Storage tips
Oils extra-virgin olive, canola and walnut oil	Store vegetable oils in the original bottles, in a cool, dark place up to 6 months. Refrigerate nut oils, and use within 3 months.
Vinegars aged balsamic, white-wine and red-wine vinegar	Keep vinegars in their original bottles. For the longest shelf-life, store them in a cool spot up to 1 year.
Grains, dried beans quick-cooking polenta; stone-ground cornmeal; oats; le puy or green lentils; black-eyed and split peas; black, pinto and cannellini beans; flageolets	Dried items, with the exception of cornmeal, can be stored in the pantry up to 1 year. To discourage pests, keep cornmeal in the freezer, up to 1 year.
Dried pasta and rice spaghetti, penne, fettuccine, lasagna and orzo; couscous; arborio, long-grain white, medium- to long-grain brown and basmati rice	Dried pasta and rice can be stored in their original packaging until opened, then transferred to airtight containers. They are best used within 1 year.
Baking needs pure vanilla extract, baking soda, baking powder, semisweet dark chocolate, dutch-process cocoa powder, unflavored gelatin, instant yeast, cornstarch	Store ingredients in airtight containers, away from heat and light sources. Extracts will last several years; leaveners lose their potency after about 1 year, and should be discarded on expiration dates.
Sugars granulated white, superfine, light and dark brown, and confectioners' sugar; light corn syrup; molasses; pure maple syrup and honey	Humidity can make solid sugars lumpy, so be sure to keep them in well-sealed containers in a cool, dry spot. Double-wrap brown sugars to keep them moist. Store syrups at room temperature in their original containers up to 1 year.
Flours all-purpose white, whole-wheat, cake (not self-rising), and almond flour	Store wheat flours in airtight containers at room temperature up to 1 year. Choose containers with wide mouths for easy scooping and measuring. Freeze almond flour up to 6 months.
Vegetables and fruits onions, garlic, dried wild mushrooms and lemons	Refrigerate lemons in a plastic bag up to 2 weeks. Keep onions and garlic in the pantry up to 1 month; dried mushrooms can be kept for several months.
Nuts and dried fruit pecan and walnut halves, almonds, hazelnuts, raisins, golden raisins, currants, dried apricots and figs, sun-dried tomatoes, dried chiles	Nuts can turn rancid easily. To discourage this, store them in the freezer for up to 6 months. Dried fruits can be stored at room temperature 6 months to a year; keep them well-sealed to preserve freshness and prevent stickiness.
Canned and bottled Italian plum tomatoes, green and black olives, olive paste, anchovies, capers, white truffle oil, anchovy paste, chickpeas, black beans, hot sauce, mustards, Italian oil-pack tuna, low-sodium chicken stock, fruit jam	Heed expiration dates; otherwise, most canned and bottled goods can be kept, unopened, for up to 1 year. Once opened, refrigerate glass bottles; transfer unused canned goods to airtight containers and refrigerate.
Spices kosher and sea salt, black peppercorns, ground cinnamon and sticks, ground and crystallized ginger, madras curry powder, dried thyme, rosemary and oregano, ground and whole-seed cumin, whole fennel seed	Most spices will lose their potency after about 1 year, but their flavor will deteriorate faster if they're stored improperly. Keep them in airtight containers, away from heat and light. Choose an accessible drawer or cabinet or a wall-mounted rack.

Martha Stewart

Millions of consumers rely on Martha Stewart as their arbiter of style and taste and their guide to all aspects of everyday living—from cooking and entertaining to decorating and gardening. Her creative vision is behind the expansive portfolio that includes *Martha Stewart Living* and *Everyday Food* magazines, the marthastewart.com Web site, the nationally syndicated *The Martha Stewart Show*, the Martha Stewart Collection of home products exclusively at Macy's, a line of fine food products developed for Costco and more.

Steak au Poivre
Kirkland Signature
Recipes developed by Martha Stewart

2 boneless shell steaks, about 12 ounces each (1 ¼ inches thick)

3 tablespoons plus 1 teaspoon coarsely ground Kirkland Signature Tellicherry black peppercorns

2 tablespoons vegetable oil, divided

1 large shallot, minced (about ¼ cup)

2 tablespoons Cognac

1 teaspoon Dijon mustard

½ cup beef or chicken stock

⅓ cup heavy cream

1 tablespoon unsalted butter

Salt

Pat steaks dry, then coat both sides with pepper.

Heat 1 tablespoon vegetable oil in a large skillet over medium-high heat until very hot but not smoking. Add steaks to the pan and cook until seared, about 5-6 minutes per side. Transfer to a platter, tented with foil.

To make the sauce, drain the fat from the skillet and discard. Wipe out the pan with a paper towel and let it cool off the burner for 2-3 minutes. Heat the remaining 1 tablespoon vegetable oil over medium heat. Add shallots and cook until they begin to soften but not brown, about 1 minute.

Add Cognac, scraping up browned bits from the bottom of the pan with a wooden spoon, and let liquid reduce until almost completely evaporated. Stir in mustard and stock, bring to a boil and let simmer until reduced by half, about 1 ½-2 minutes. Add cream, bring to a boil and reduce until slightly thickened, about 1 minute more.

Remove the pan from the heat and add butter, swirling until completely incorporated. Season with salt to taste. Pour the sauce over the steaks and serve immediately. Makes 2 servings.

Spice-Rubbed Grilled Chicken with Parsley-Mint Sauce
Kirkland Signature

2 tablespoons Kirkland Signature Organic No-Salt Seasoning

6 boneless, skinless chicken breast halves

¼ cup Kirkland Signature extra-virgin olive oil

PARSLEY-MINT SAUCE

1 cup flat-leaf parsley leaves

½ cup fresh mint leaves

1 large garlic clove

⅓ cup water

¼ cup Kirkland Signature extra-virgin olive oil

2 tablespoons fresh lemon juice

Kirkland Signature Mediterranean sea salt, coarse grind (optional)

Rub no-salt seasoning onto both sides of chicken breasts. Brush olive oil over chicken.

Heat grill to medium. Grill chicken in a single layer, turning it when grill marks show and chicken is nicely colored, about 5 minutes. Continue cooking until an instant-read thermometer inserted into the chicken reaches 160°F, about 4 more minutes.

Meanwhile, prepare the parsley-mint sauce by combining parsley, mint, garlic, water, olive oil and lemon juice in a blender or a food processor. Puree until smooth, then season with coarse sea salt as desired.

Let the chicken stand for 5 minutes. Spread the parsley-mint sauce on top before serving. Makes 6 servings.

Tip: The parsley-mint sauce can be covered and refrigerated overnight.

Sea Salt Caramels
Kirkland Signature

Vegetable-oil spray
Parchment paper
4 cups heavy cream
2 cups light corn syrup
4 cups sugar
¾ cup (1 ½ sticks) unsalted
    butter, cut into pieces

1 teaspoon vanilla extract
2 teaspoons Kirkland Signature
    Mediterranean sea salt,
    medium grind
2 teaspoons Kirkland Signature
    Mediterranean sea salt,
    coarse grind

Spray a 16 ½-by-11 ¾-inch baking pan (a half-sheet pan) with vegetable-oil spray; line with parchment paper and spray the parchment. Set aside.

Put cream, corn syrup, sugar and butter in a large stockpot. Bring to a boil over high heat, stirring to melt butter and dissolve sugar, about 10 minutes. Cook over medium-high heat, stirring often, until temperature reaches 248°F (firm-ball stage) on a candy thermometer, about 20 minutes.

Remove from the heat and stir in vanilla and medium-grind sea salt until combined. Immediately pour into the prepared pan without scraping the pot. Sprinkle coarse-grind sea salt in an even layer over the top. Let stand, uncovered, at room temperature for 24 hours without moving.

Using a large knife, cut around outside of caramel in pan. Lift caramel out of pan and remove parchment paper. Cut into 1-by-1 ¼-inch pieces, or other shapes. Wrap each piece in cellophane or waxed paper so they keep their shape. Makes about 150 caramels.

Note: The Kirkland Signature Mediterranean sea salt grinder can be conveniently adjusted from a coarse grind to a fine grind.

Sandra Lee

Sandra Lee is an internationally acclaimed home and style expert with an Emmy-nominated TV show, *Semi-Homemade Cooking with Sandra Lee*, on the Food Network. She has 14 books to her credit, including three new titles: *Semi-Homemade Money Saving Meals, Desserts 2* and *Fast-Fix Family Favorites* (some available at costco.com). Her trademark 70/30 Semi-Homemade® philosophy—combine 70 percent store-bought products with 30 percent fresh ingredients or creative touches for a great meal—perfectly suits today's busy lifestyles and tight budgets. For more, see *www.SemiHomemade.com*.

Key Lime-
Grilled Chicken

Chef's Choice

Key Lime-Grilled Chicken
Gold Kist Farms
Recipes developed by Sandra Lee Semi-Homemade

KEY LIME SAUCE

1 stick (¹/₂ cup) butter

¹/₄ cup key lime juice

¹/₄ cup chili sauce

2 teaspoons all-purpose poultry seasoning mix

4 pounds Gold Kist Farms* meaty chicken pieces (breasts or thighs)

1 tablespoon all-purpose poultry seasoning mix

Set up grill for direct cooking over medium heat. Oil grate when ready to start cooking.

To prepare Key Lime Sauce, melt butter in a small saucepan over medium heat. Stir in lime juice, chili sauce and 2 teaspoons poultry seasoning mix. Cook for 1 minute. Remove from the heat; set aside.

Season chicken with 1 tablespoon poultry seasoning mix. Place chicken on the hot, oiled grill and cook for 18-22 minutes per side, or until chicken is no longer pink and juices run clear (180°F), basting with Key Lime Sauce every few minutes until the last 2 minutes of cooking. Discard any remaining sauce. Makes 4 servings.

Tip: To cook indoors, preheat broiler. Prepare chicken and Key Lime Sauce as directed. Place chicken on a foil-lined baking sheet or broiler pan. Broil chicken 6-8 inches from heat source for about 15-20 minutes per side, or until chicken is no longer pink and juices run clear (180°F), basting with Key Lime Sauce every few minutes until the last 2 minutes of cooking. Discard any remaining sauce.

* Brands may vary by region; substitute a similar product.

Drunken Wings
Gold Kist Farms

¹/₃ cup light rum

¹/₃ cup honey

¹/₄ cup soy sauce

2 tablespoons Thai chili sauce

1 ³/₄-ounce packet stir-fry seasoning

2 teaspoons crushed garlic

4 pounds Gold Kist Farms* chicken wings

3 scallions, finely chopped (optional)

¹/₄ cup chopped peanuts (optional)

In a large bowl, combine rum, honey, soy sauce, chili sauce, stir-fry seasoning and garlic. Add chicken wings, tossing to coat. Cover with plastic wrap and marinate in the refrigerator for at least 3 hours, preferably overnight.

Set up grill for direct cooking over medium-high heat. Oil grate when ready to start cooking. Let wings stand at room temperature for 30 minutes. Place on the hot, oiled grill. Cook for 12-18 minutes, or until cooked through, turning occasionally.

Transfer chicken to a platter. Sprinkle with chopped scallions and peanuts. Makes 4 servings.

Tip: To cook indoors, prepare chicken as directed. Preheat broiler. Place chicken on a foil-lined baking sheet or broiling pan. Broil 6-8 inches from heat source for 12-15 minutes, or until cooked through, turning occasionally.

* Brands may vary by region; substitute a similar product.

Balsamic-Marinated Chicken Under Bricks
Gold Kist Farms

4 Gold Kist Farms* boneless, skinless chicken breast halves

1 cup balsamic vinaigrette

½ cup balsamic vinegar

¼ cup chopped fresh parsley

2 tablespoons frozen orange juice concentrate, thawed

1 tablespoon Italian seasoning

2 teaspoons crushed garlic

2 bricks wrapped in aluminum foil

Rinse chicken under cold water and pat dry with paper towels. Flatten the chicken with a mallet.

Place chicken in a large ziplock bag. Add balsamic vinaigrette, vinegar, parsley, orange juice concentrate, Italian seasoning and garlic. Squeeze air out of the bag and seal. Gently massage the bag to combine. Marinate in the refrigerator for 1-4 hours.

Set up grill for direct grilling over medium-high heat. Oil grate when ready to start cooking. Let chicken stand at room temperature for 30 minutes.

Remove chicken from the marinade; discard marinade. Place chicken on the hot, oiled grill and place foil-wrapped bricks on top. Cook for 3-4 minutes per side, or until chicken is no longer pink and juices run clear (170°F). Makes 4 servings.

Tip: To cook indoors, omit the foil-wrapped bricks. Prepare chicken as directed. Preheat broiler. Place chicken on a foil-lined baking sheet or broiler pan. Broil 6-8 inches from heat source for 5-6 minutes per side, or until chicken is no longer pink and juices run clear (170°F). Do not overcook.

* Brands may vary by region; substitute a similar product.

Paula Deen

Paula Deen is a self-made success story who learned the secrets of Southern cooking from her mother and grand-mother. She is the author of numerous cookbooks, including *The Lady & Sons Savannah Country Cookbook, The Lady & Sons Just Desserts, Paula Deen & Friends* and *Paula Deen Celebrates!* (some available at costco.com). Her show on Food Network is *Paula's Home Cooking.*

Honey Sesame Pork Chops
Farmland/Smithfield
Recipes developed by Paula Deen

MARINADE

- 2 tablespoons plus 2 teaspoons light soy sauce
- 1 garlic clove, crushed
- 2 teaspoons dry sherry
- 1 tablespoon plus 1 teaspoon honey
- 1/8 teaspoon five-spice powder
- 3/4 teaspoon toasted sesame oil
- 3/4 teaspoon sesame seeds
- 8 Farmland/Smithfield* center-cut pork rib chops, trimmed

To prepare the marinade, combine all ingredients in a bowl and stir thoroughly.

Place pork chops in a shallow dish and add the marinade. Cover and refrigerate for several hours or overnight.

Preheat oven to 350°F.

Place pork chops on a wire rack over a baking dish. Bake for about 35 minutes, brushing with marinade occasionally, or until tender (internal temperature should be 145°F). Makes 4 servings.

* Brands may vary by region; substitute a similar product.

Bacon, Napa Cabbage and Carrot Slaw with Toasted Sesame Seeds
Smithfield/Farmer's

- 3 carrots, shredded
- 1 small head Napa cabbage, shredded
- 1 bunch green onions, thinly sliced
- 1/4 cup coarsely chopped fresh cilantro leaves
- 2 tablespoons fresh lemon juice
- 1 tablespoon white-wine vinegar
- 1 teaspoon sugar
- 1 tablespoon toasted sesame oil
- 1/2 teaspoon hot pepper sauce
- 1/3 cup vegetable oil
- 1/2 cup crisp-cooked and finely diced Kirkland Signature* center cut bacon
- 1/4 cup toasted sesame seeds

In a large bowl, combine carrots, cabbage, green onions and cilantro.

Combine all remaining ingredients except sesame seeds in a small bowl and whisk until blended.

Add dressing to the cabbage mixture and toss to coat. Sprinkle with sesame seeds. Makes 4 servings.

* Brands may vary by region; substitute a similar product.

Baby Back Ribs
Curly's

2 pounds Curly's* baby back ribs
1/4 cup fermented black bean paste
1 teaspoon minced garlic
1 teaspoon minced fresh ginger
1 small red chili pepper, seeded and chopped
1 tablespoon brown sugar

2 tablespoons chicken broth or water
1/3 cup high-quality soy sauce
1/4 cup hoisin sauce
Toasted sesame oil
2 green onions, chopped into 1/2-inch lengths

Preheat oven to 350°F.

Remove ribs from the package and scrape off as much sauce as possible. Reserve this sauce in a saucepot. Cut the ribs into 2- to 4-rib sections and place in a shallow ovenproof dish.

In a separate bowl, mash fermented beans with garlic, ginger, chili and sugar. Add this mixture to the saucepot with the reserved sauce. Heat the mixture over medium heat, stirring often, until aromatic. Add chicken broth, soy sauce and hoisin sauce and bring to a boil, stirring often so that the mixture does not stick and burn. Reduce the heat and simmer for 5 minutes.

Remove the saucepot from the heat and stir in a few drops of sesame oil. Pour the warmed sauce over the ribs. Cover with foil and heat in the oven for about 25-35 minutes, or until the ribs are heated through.

Arrange the ribs on a platter, garnish with green onions and serve. Makes 4 servings.

Tip: Give the dish a little more zip by adding Paula Deen Hot Sauce or hot chili oil to taste to the saucepot after removing from the heat and before spooning over the ribs.

* Brands may vary by region; substitute a similar product.

Steven Raichlen

Multi-award-winning author, journalist, cooking teacher and TV host Steven Raichlen is the man who gave barbecue a college education. His bestselling *Barbecue! Bible* (Workman, 1998) cookbook series (more than 4 million copies in print) and *Barbecue University* television show on PBS have virtually reinvented American barbecue. Raichlen's new PBS television series, *Primal Grill*, premiered in May 2008, alongside the publication of the 10th-anniversary edition of *The Barbecue! Bible* (available at costco.com). All in all, Raichlen has written 28 books. He lives with his wife, Barbara, in Coconut Grove, Florida.

Grilled Italian Sausage with Polenta and Grilled Pepper Salad

Grilled Italian Sausage with Polenta and Grilled Pepper Salad
Tarantino
Recipes developed by Steven Raichlen

PEPPER SALAD

2 red bell peppers

2 yellow or orange bell peppers

2 green bell peppers

DRESSING

1 garlic clove, chopped

1/2 teaspoon coarse salt (kosher or sea), or more to taste

1 tablespoon balsamic vinegar

1 tablespoon lemon juice

4 tablespoons extra-virgin olive oil

2 tablespoons chopped fresh flat-leaf parsley or slivered fresh basil

16 Tarantino* mild Italian sausages

POLENTA

2-3 tablespoons olive oil

1 garlic clove, minced

1 tablespoon chopped fresh rosemary or another herb (optional)

1 1 1/2-pound package commercially prepared cooked polenta, cut in 1/2-inch-thick slices

1 cup freshly grated Parmesan cheese

Freshly ground black pepper

Set up the grill for direct grilling and preheat to medium-high.

Grill peppers until the skins are charred on all sides, 4-6 minutes per side (16-24 minutes in all), turning with tongs. Transfer peppers to a baking dish, cover with plastic wrap and let cool to room temperature, about 20 minutes.

To prepare the dressing, place garlic and salt in a nonreactive mixing bowl and mash to a paste with the back of a wooden spoon. Add vinegar and lemon juice and whisk until the salt is dissolved. Whisk in oil and parsley.

Using the tip of a paring knife, scrape the burnt skin off the peppers and cut the flesh off the core. Cut the peppers into quarters or strips and arrange on a platter, alternating pieces of different colors. Stir the dressing and spoon it over the peppers.

Grill the sausages 2-3 minutes per side (8-12 minutes total), or until a thermometer inserted in the sausage (parallel to the grill) registers 160°F. Place the hot sausages on top of the prepared peppers.

To prepare the polenta, combine olive oil, garlic and rosemary in a small bowl. Brush polenta slices with the oil; grill them 2-4 minutes per side, rotating a quarter turn after 1 minute for a crosshatch pattern of grill marks. Remove to a plate or platter, and immediately sprinkle Parmesan on top; a few grinds of black pepper are optional. Serve immediately. Makes 8 servings.

Tip: You can serve the pepper salad right away with the sausages and polenta, or let it sit for a few hours (refrigerated) to let the flavors blend. Bring it to room temperature before topping it with the sausages.

Recipes from Steven Raichlen's BBQ USA *and* How to Grill *(Workman Publishing).*
* Brands may vary by region; substitute a similar product.

Beer-Simmered Grilled Sausages
Tarantino

8 Tarantino* mild Italian sausages

1 onion, thinly sliced

3 cups beer, as needed

1 tablespoon vegetable oil

Mustard

Prick each sausage a half-dozen times.

Arrange onion slices on the bottom of a sauté pan just large enough to hold all the sausages.

Place sausages on top and add beer and water to cover (the ratio should be about 3 parts beer to 1 part water). Place the pan over medium heat and gradually bring the liquid to a simmer, not a rapid boil. Poach the sausages until half-cooked, 4-5 minutes.

Set up the grill for direct grilling and preheat to medium-high. Brush and oil the grill grate. Lightly brush the sausages on all sides with oil and place on the hot grate.

Grill the sausages until the casings are crisp and nicely browned, 4-6 minutes per side. To test for doneness, insert a metal skewer into the center of a sausage; it should come out hot to the touch.

Transfer the sausages to plates and let rest for 3 minutes. Serve with plenty of mustard. Makes 8 servings.

* Brands may vary by region; substitute a similar product.

French Toast on the Grill with Sausages
Tarantino

8 Tarantino* breakfast
  sausage links

FRENCH TOAST
2 large eggs
2 tablespoons maple syrup
1 cup milk
1 teaspoon pure vanilla extract
8 slices pound cake (1/2 inch thick)

Confectioners' sugar
4 cups fresh blueberries, raspberries
  and/or other berries (optional)
Maple syrup (optional)

Set up the grill for direct grilling and preheat to medium-high. Brush and oil the grill grate.

Grill the sausages, turning frequently, until the casings are crisp and nicely browned, about 5 minutes. Move the sausages to the perimeter of the grill or to a warming rack.

To prepare the French toast, place eggs and maple syrup in a large, wide bowl. Using a whisk, beat just to mix. Whisk in milk and vanilla.

Dip each slice of pound cake in the egg mixture, letting it soak for 2-4 seconds per side. Place the cake slices on the hot grate on the diagonal and grill until lightly browned, 2-4 minutes per side.

Transfer the French toast slices to a platter and sprinkle with confectioners' sugar. Serve with fresh berries and/or maple syrup. Makes 4 servings.

* Brands may vary by region; substitute a similar product.

Ina Garten

In 1978, Ina Garten left her job as a budget analyst at the White House to pursue her dream: operating a specialty food store in the Hamptons. Since opening The Barefoot Contessa, Garten has gone on to star in a Food Network show of the same name and written the phenomenally successful *Barefoot Contessa* cookbook series, including her latest: *Barefoot Contessa Back to Basics* (available at costco.com). She lives in East Hampton, New York, with her husband, Jeffrey.

Rack of Lamb
Australian Lamb

Recipe developed by Ina Garten from
Barefoot Contessa Parties!

1 ¹/2 tablespoons kosher salt
2 tablespoons minced fresh rosemary leaves
3 garlic cloves, minced
¹/2 cup Dijon mustard
1 tablespoon balsamic vinegar
2 Australian racks of lamb (7-8 ribs each)

In the bowl of a food processor fitted with a steel blade, process salt, rosemary and garlic until they're as finely minced as possible. Add mustard and vinegar and process for 1 minute.

Place lamb in a roasting or sheet pan with the ribs curving down, and coat the tops with the mustard mixture. Allow to stand for 1 hour at room temperature.

Preheat the oven to 450°F.

Roast the lamb for exactly 20 minutes for rare or 25 minutes for medium-rare. Remove from the oven and cover with aluminum foil. Allow to sit for 15 minutes, then cut into individual ribs and serve. Makes 6 servings.

THE
AUSTRALIAN LAMB
COMPANY INC.

Grilled Australian Lamb Loin Chops
Australian Lamb

1 6.5-ounce jar sun-dried tomatoes in oil, sliced into thin strips (reserve the oil)
1 medium yellow onion, sliced julienne (about 2 cups)
2 garlic cloves, minced
1 tablespoon capers, rinsed and chopped
1 ¹/2 cups chicken stock, divided
1 cup toasted pine nuts, divided
4 anchovy fillets
Zest from 1 lemon
1 tablespoon red wine vinegar
2 tablespoons chopped fresh basil
2 tablespoons chopped fresh parsley
Salt
Black pepper, fresh cracked
8 Australian Lamb loin chops

Preheat a skillet over medium-high heat. Add 3 tablespoons of the oil from the sun-dried tomatoes and the onions. Cook onions until translucent. Add sun-dried tomatoes, garlic, capers and 1 cup of the chicken stock, and simmer for 5 minutes.

Transfer half of the sun-dried tomato mixture to a food processor and the other half to a small mixing bowl.

In the food processor, add ¹/2 cup of the toasted pine nuts, anchovies, lemon zest and vinegar. Pulse to coarsely chop but not fully puree the tomatoes. Add remaining chicken stock as needed.

Combine the mixtures and stir in basil, parsley and remaining pine nuts; season to taste with salt and pepper. Keep warm.

Season the lamb with salt and pepper. Grill the chops to desired doneness, about 4 minutes per side for medium. Transfer to a plate or platter.

Spoon 2 heaping tablespoonfuls of the sun-dried tomato mixture over the top of each lamb chop. Makes 4 servings.

Herb-Roasted Lamb
Australian Lamb
Recipe developed by Ina Garten from
Barefoot Contessa Family Style

12 large unpeeled garlic
   cloves, divided

1 tablespoon chopped fresh
   rosemary leaves

Kosher salt

Freshly ground black pepper

2 tablespoons unsalted
   butter, melted

1 4- to 5-pound butterflied
   Australian leg of lamb

4-5 pounds small unpeeled
   potatoes (16-20 potatoes)

2 tablespoons good olive oil

Preheat oven to 450°F. Place the oven rack in the lower third of the oven so the lamb will sit in the middle of the oven.

Peel 6 of the garlic cloves and place them in the bowl of a food processor fitted with the steel blade. Add rosemary, 1 tablespoon salt, 1 teaspoon pepper and butter. Process until the garlic and rosemary are finely minced.

Thoroughly coat the top and sides of the lamb with the rosemary mixture. Allow to sit at room temperature for 30 minutes to 1 hour.

Toss potatoes and remaining unpeeled garlic in a bowl with olive oil and sprinkle with salt. Place in the bottom of a large roasting pan. Place the lamb on top of the potatoes and roast for 1-1 1/4 hours, or until the internal temperature of the lamb is 135°F (rare) or 145°F (medium).

Remove from the oven and put the lamb on a platter; cover tightly with aluminum foil. Allow the lamb to rest for about 20 minutes. Slice and serve with the potatoes. Makes 10 servings.

Jessica Seinfeld

Jessica Seinfeld is a bestselling author, the wife of a famous comedian and a devoted advocate for families in need. Her first book, *Deceptively Delicious: Simple Secrets to Get Your Kids Eating Good Food* (HarperCollins, 2007, available at costco.com), was a number-one *New York Times* bestseller. She is the founder and president of Baby Buggy, a nonprofit organization that delivers donations of new and gently used baby clothing and equipment to New York City families in need. She lives in Manhattan with her husband, comedian Jerry Seinfeld, and their three children.

Fantastic Alfredo

Garofalo

Fantastic Alfredo

Garofalo

Recipe developed by Jessica Seinfeld

12 ounces Garofalo*
   penne pasta

2 tablespoons trans-fat-free
   soft tub margarine

2 garlic cloves, minced

2 tablespoons whole
   wheat flour

1 cup fat-free milk

1 cup grated reduced-fat
   (2%) sharp white Cheddar
   or part-skim mozzarella

$^1/_2$ cup cauliflower puree

$^1/_4$ cup grated
   Parmesan cheese

$^1/_2$ teaspoon salt

$^1/_4$ teaspoon freshly
   ground black pepper

$^1/_4$ teaspoon sweet paprika

2 sprigs fresh basil, for
   garnish (optional)

Cook pasta according to package directions. Reserve $^1/_2$ cup of the cooking water, then strain pasta. Set aside.

Heat margarine in a large skillet with deep sides over medium heat. When the margarine foams, add garlic. Cook for 1-2 minutes, or until garlic is fragrant but does not brown.

Add flour and cook for 4-5 minutes, whisking the flour into the margarine until a smooth paste forms.

Whisk in $^1/_4$ cup of the milk at a time until the milk is absorbed and a creamy sauce starts to form. Once all the milk is incorporated, bring the sauce to a slow boil, whisking for 1 additional minute. Stir in Cheddar or mozzarella, cauliflower puree and Parmesan, mixing until smooth, about 1-2 minutes. Add salt, pepper, paprika and pasta. Toss to coat. Add a little of the reserved pasta water if the mixture is too thick.

Top with basil sprigs and serve immediately. Makes 4 servings.

* Brands may vary by region; substitute a similar product.

Tri-Color Farfalle Chicken Caesar Salad

Garofalo

8 ounces Garofalo*
   tri-color farfalle pasta

1 cup Caesar salad
   dressing, divided

6 ounces shaved
   Parmesan
   cheese, divided

6 cups chopped
   romaine or Italian
   lettuce blend

4 cups Roma tomatoes
   cut into wedges

Freshly ground
   black pepper

$^3/_4$ cup Caesar croutons

2 medium chicken
   breasts, grilled
   and sliced

Cook pasta according to package directions. Drain and stir to separate pasta. Do not rinse.

Combine pasta and $^1/_2$ cup Caesar salad dressing in a salad bowl. Cover and refrigerate for 1 hour.

Add half of the Parmesan and all of the lettuce, tomatoes, ground black pepper and croutons to the chilled pasta. Mix well.

To serve, place sliced chicken on top of the salad, sprinkle with the remaining Parmesan and drizzle with the remaining salad dressing. Makes 8 servings.

* Brands may vary by region; substitute a similar product.

Pasta with Bolognese Sauce
Garofalo
Recipe developed by Jessica Seinfeld

1 medium onion
2 garlic cloves
Nonstick cooking spray
1 tablespoon olive oil
3 carrots
1 celery stalk
1/2 pound lean ground sirloin
1/2 pound lean ground turkey
1/2 teaspoon salt

1/8 teaspoon pepper
1 28-ounce can crushed tomatoes
1 cup reduced-fat low-sodium
    chicken or beef broth
1 tablespoon sugar
1/2 cup sweet potato puree
2 tablespoons grated
    Parmesan cheese
1 package Garofalo* spaghetti

Put onion and garlic in a food processor and finely chop (or chop by hand).

Coat a large nonstick skillet with cooking spray and set over medium-high heat.

When the skillet is hot, add olive oil, then onion and garlic; cook until onion and garlic begin to soften, 2-3 minutes.

Meanwhile, put carrots and celery in the food processor and finely chop; add to the skillet and cook 3-4 minutes longer.

Increase the heat to high, add ground meats and break into small chunks with a wooden spoon. Add salt and pepper and cook until the meat begins to brown, 3-4 minutes. Add tomatoes, broth and sugar. Reduce the heat to low, cover and simmer, stirring occasionally, for 30 minutes. Stir in sweet potato puree and Parmesan.

Cook pasta in a large pot of salted boiling water according to package directions until al dente. Drain in a colander, then return the pasta to the pot. Pour the warm sauce over the pasta (toss if desired). Makes 4 servings.

Tip: Try this recipe with Garofalo whole wheat organic spaghetti, available at select Costco locations.

* Brands may vary by region; substitute a similar product.

Ellie Krieger

Ellie Krieger is the host of the popular Food Network show *Healthy Appetite* and author of the *New York Times* bestseller *The Food You Crave* (The Taunton Press, 2008, available at costco.com). A registered dietitian, she has a master's degree in nutrition from Columbia University and did her undergraduate work at Cornell University. Krieger is a regular contributor to *Parenting* and *Fitness* magazines and lives in New York City.

Balsamic Chicken with Baby Spinach and Couscous
Foster Farms
Recipe developed by Ellie Krieger

3 tablespoons olive oil, divided

4 Foster Farms* boneless, skinless chicken breast halves, pounded between 2 sheets of waxed paper to 1/2-inch thickness

1/4 teaspoon salt, plus more to taste

1/4 teaspoon freshly ground black pepper, plus more to taste

3 garlic cloves, chopped (about 1 tablespoon)

8 ounces baby spinach leaves (about 8 cups lightly packed)

2 tablespoons balsamic vinegar

1/2 cup low-sodium chicken broth

1 cup canned no-salt-added chopped tomatoes, with their juices

2 cups hot cooked whole-wheat couscous (from about 3/4 cup uncooked)

Heat 1 tablespoon olive oil in a large skillet over medium-high heat. Season chicken on both sides with salt and pepper. Add chicken to the pan and cook until browned and just cooked through, about 4 minutes per side, or until the chicken reaches an internal temperature of 165°F. Remove the chicken to a plate.

Add remaining 2 tablespoons olive oil to the pan; add garlic and cook for 1 minute. Add spinach and cook just until wilted, 1-2 minutes. Season with salt and pepper, then transfer the spinach to a bowl and set aside.

Add vinegar, chicken broth and tomatoes to the pan and stir, scraping any browned bits off the bottom. Bring to a simmer and cook until the sauce is slightly thickened, 3-5 minutes.

Divide the couscous between 4 serving plates. Top with some of the spinach, then a piece of chicken and the balsamic-tomato sauce. Makes 4 servings.

* Brands may vary by region; substitute a similar product.

Rosemary Thighs
Foster Farms

1 tablespoon olive oil

1/4 cup dry red wine

1 teaspoon chopped fresh rosemary or 1/2 teaspoon dried

1 teaspoon chopped fresh sage or 1/2 teaspoon dried

1 tablespoon minced shallot or green onion

1/4 teaspoon seasoned salt

1/4 teaspoon white or black pepper

Nonstick cooking spray

6 Foster Farms* boneless, skinless chicken thighs

Preheat oven to 400°F.

In a medium stainless steel or glass bowl, whisk together olive oil, wine, rosemary, sage, shallot, salt and pepper. Set aside.

Spray a shallow glass or enameled baking dish with cooking spray. Place chicken thighs in a single layer in the prepared dish. Pour rosemary-wine mixture over chicken, and cover tightly with foil. Bake for 30 minutes. Remove the foil and turn the thighs.

Continue to bake, uncovered, basting several times, for 20-25 minutes, or until the internal temperature is 180°F. Remove the chicken to a warm platter. Reduce pan juices, if desired, and pour over the chicken. Makes 6 servings.

* Brands may vary by region; substitute a similar product.

Stuffed Turkey Burgers
Foster Farms
Recipe developed by Ellie Krieger

1 1/4 **pounds Foster Farms*** **ground turkey**

1/2 **cup chopped roasted red peppers (drained and rinsed if from a jar)**

1/2 **cup (2 ounces) shredded part-skim mozzarella cheese**

1/4 **teaspoon salt**

Freshly ground black pepper

4 whole-wheat buns

Preheat the broiler or prepare the grill.

Divide turkey into 4 equal-sized rounds. Make 2 equal-sized patties out of each round, for 8 patties total.

Sprinkle one side of 4 of the patties with 2 tablespoons each of roasted red peppers and cheese, and top with remaining patties, working the turkey around the edges to seal the burgers closed.

Sprinkle the patties with the salt and a few grinds of pepper. Grill or broil until cooked through, about 5 minutes per side. Serve on the buns. Makes 4 servings.

* Brands may vary by region; substitute a similar product.

Susan Lamb Parenti

Susan Lamb Parenti is a seasoned and impassioned food professional, bringing more than 20 years' experience in the food world to JBS Swift's product development team. She heads Parenti Partners, a boutique culinary consulting practice specializing in comprehensive food marketing support services. Parenti previously served as director of the Beef & Veal Culinary Center for the National Cattlemen's Beef Association. She and her husband reside in Park Ridge, Illinois, with their four children.

Vesuvio-Style
Pork Tenderloin

Vesuvio-Style Pork Tenderloin
Swift
Recipes developed by Susan Lamb Parenti

1 tablespoon olive oil

3 medium baking potatoes, scrubbed, each cut lengthwise into 6 wedges

2 pork tenderloins, about 2 1/2 inches thick

1 lemon, thinly sliced

1/2 cup frozen peas, defrosted

Salt

SEASONING

3 large garlic cloves, minced

1 1/2 teaspoons dried oregano, crushed

1/2 teaspoon sea salt

1/2 teaspoon ground pepper

Preheat oven to 425°F.

Combine seasoning ingredients. Mix 1 teaspoon of the seasoning with olive oil; toss with potato wedges. Spread in a single layer in a shallow baking pan.

Press remaining seasoning evenly onto pork tenderloins; place in a roasting pan. Place lemon slices around pork.

Roast tenderloins and potatoes, uncovered, for 15 minutes. Turn potato wedges over. Continue roasting 10-15 minutes longer, or until pork reaches medium (155°F) doneness. Remove tenderloins to a carving board; let rest.

Add peas to potatoes; continue roasting until potatoes are fork-tender, about 5 minutes. Season to taste with salt.

Carve tenderloins into 1/2-inch-thick slices. Serve with potatoes, peas and lemon slices. Makes 4-6 servings.

Orange-Jalapeño Glazed Back Ribs
Swift

3 racks pork back ribs (about 8 pounds)

Sea salt and pepper

ORANGE-JALAPEÑO GLAZE

1 18-ounce jar orange marmalade (1 3/4 cups)

1/2 cup chopped, seeded jalapeño peppers (3 peppers)

1/4 cup distilled white vinegar

4 garlic cloves, minced

1 teaspoon dried rosemary, crushed

1/2 teaspoon sea salt

Preheat oven to 325°F.

Remove the thin papery membrane from the underside of rib racks (if present): Slide the tip of a small knife under the membrane at the third rib and loosen until you can peel it off. Cut each rack crosswise in half; season to taste with salt and pepper.

To prepare the glaze, combine all ingredients in a small saucepan; heat to simmering. Cook, uncovered, over medium-low heat, stirring occasionally, for 10 minutes. Let cool slightly.

Place ribs in a single layer in 1 large or 2 small roasting pans. Cover the pans tightly with aluminum foil. Cook in the oven until the meat is fork-tender, about 1 1/2 hours. Remove ribs from the oven; pour off drippings.

Increase oven setting to 375°F. Brush ribs with glaze. Return to the oven and cook, uncovered, until the ribs are glazed, watching carefully, about 10 minutes. Makes 6 servings.

Tip: To cook ribs on the grill, prepare grill for indirect grilling. Place ribs on grid over a drip pan (or over off burners for gas grills). Grill, covered, until the meat is fork-tender, about 1 1/2 hours. Brush with glaze during the last 5 minutes.

Note: Wear disposable plastic gloves when handling jalapeño peppers, and do not touch face or eyes with hands.

In The Kitchen The Costco Way

Grilled Pepper-Crusted Strip Steaks and Creamy Garlic Spinach
Swift

PEPPERY RUB

1 teaspoon lemon pepper

1/2 teaspoon sea salt

1/2 teaspoon freshly ground black pepper

1/4 teaspoon ground chipotle pepper

4 beef top loin (strip) steaks, 1 1/4 inches thick

CREAMY GARLIC SPINACH

1 16-ounce package fresh baby spinach

1 5.2-ounce package spreadable garlic and herb cheese (such as Boursin), at room temperature

1 tablespoon cream or milk

Combine the rub ingredients; press evenly onto steaks. Place steaks on grill over medium, ash-covered coals. Grill, uncovered, about 15-18 minutes for medium-rare to medium doneness, turning occasionally.

Meanwhile, prepare the spinach. Bring a large pot of water to a boil. Add spinach; remove from the heat. Stir just until spinach is wilted. Drain well, pressing out excess liquid. Wipe the pot dry; return spinach to the pot. Add cheese and cream; stir until cheese melts and coats spinach evenly.

Serve the steaks with the spinach. Makes 4 servings.

Myra Goodman

Myra Goodman and her husband, Drew, founded Earthbound Farm in their Carmel Valley, California, backyard 24 years ago. Living on a farm, Goodman developed a passion for cooking with the healthiest, freshest and most flavorful ingredients possible. That passion is reflected in her beautiful and inspiring cookbook, *Food to Live By: The Earthbound Farm Organic Cookbook* (Workman Publishing, 2006, available at costco.com).

Mixed Baby Greens Salad with Oranges, Pecans and Blue Cheese
Earthbound Farm

Recipes developed by Myra Goodman

6 cups (tightly packed, approx. 5 ounces) Earthbound Farm* Organic Mixed Baby Greens Organic

2 oranges, peeled, segmented, juice reserved

1/2 cup pecans, toasted and coarsely chopped

2 ounces blue cheese, crumbled

DRESSING

1 teaspoon minced shallot

1/2 teaspoon minced garlic

1 tablespoon red wine vinegar

1 tablespoon orange juice

2 tablespoons olive oil

2 tablespoons canola oil

1 teaspoon salt

1/4 teaspoon ground pepper

Place salad greens in a large bowl.

In a separate small bowl, whisk dressing ingredients together until well blended.

Add the dressing to the salad greens a little at a time and toss lightly.

Top with orange segments, pecans and blue cheese. Serve immediately. Makes 4 servings.

* Brands may vary by region; substitute a similar product.

Earthbound Farm.
ORGANIC
Food to live by.

Harvest Basket Apple Crisp
Earthbound Farm

FILLING

2 6-ounce bags (total 12 ounces) Earthbound Farm* Organic Apple Slices Organic

2 tablespoons flour

2 teaspoons ground cinnamon

1/2 cup sugar

3 tablespoons butter, melted

TOPPING

1/2 cup flour

3 tablespoons brown sugar

1/4 cup old-fashioned oats

3/4 teaspoon ground cinnamon

Pinch of salt

3 tablespoons butter, cut into small pieces

3 tablespoons coarsely chopped walnuts

Vanilla ice cream or whipped cream (optional)

Preheat oven to 350°F.

To prepare the filling, prick apple slices with a fork. Combine flour, cinnamon and sugar in a mixing bowl. Add apples and stir to coat well. Add melted butter, mixing until well covered. Pour into a shallow 9-inch square baking dish. Cover with foil and bake for 40 minutes.

To prepare the topping, mix all ingredients together by hand, until the mixture is crumbly.

Remove the apple filling from the oven, remove the foil and cover apples evenly with the topping. Bake, uncovered, for an additional 20 minutes.

Serve with ice cream or whipped cream. Makes 6 servings.

* Brands may vary by region; substitute a similar product.

Mark J. Del Priore

Mark J. Del Priore is a graduate of the Culinary Institute of America and has more than 37 years of experience in the restaurant and hospitality industry. He has served as a chef, corporate chef's adviser and general manager in numerous leading establishments, and is currently general manager at St. Andrews Country Club in Boca Raton, Florida. His favorite saying is "I love to eat, but I live to cook."

Veal Cutlets Milanese
Plume De Veau
Recipes developed by Mark J. Del Priore

8 thin slices Plume De Veau* veal scallopini, about 1 ¹/₂ pounds

4 tablespoons flour

Salt and freshly ground pepper

3 eggs, beaten

1 cup Italian-flavored dry bread crumbs

¹/₄ cup olive oil

16 ounces prepared bruschetta topping

Pound veal with a mallet to uniform thickness.

Season flour with salt and pepper to taste. Dredge veal all over with flour, shaking off excess.

Dip veal in eggs and then in bread crumbs, covering completely.

Heat ¹/₄ inch olive oil in a heavy skillet over medium-high heat. Fry breaded cutlets in oil, turning once (about 2 minutes per side). Remove to a warm plate.

Spoon bruschetta topping over the cutlets when ready to serve. Makes 4 servings.

* Brands may vary by region; substitute a similar product.

Veal Chops au Poivre
Plume De Veau

1 tablespoon black peppercorns

4 Plume De Veau* veal chops (rib or loin)

1 teaspoon salt

2 tablespoons olive oil, divided

¹/₄ cup Cognac

¹/₃ cup heavy cream

Coarsely crush peppercorns by gently pounding once or twice with a mallet or heavy skillet.

Pat veal chops dry and sprinkle with salt and peppercorns, pressing to help them adhere.

Heat 1 tablespoon olive oil in a heavy skillet over moderate heat. Add 2 chops to the skillet and cook, turning over when browned on one side (4-6 minutes total). Transfer to a plate and wipe out the skillet. Cook remaining 2 chops in 1 tablespoon olive oil. (Do not wipe out the skillet after the second batch.)

Remove the skillet from the heat and add Cognac. Return to the heat and boil, scraping up any browned bits, until reduced by half, about 1 minute. Add cream and any veal juices accumulated on the plate to the skillet, then boil, stirring occasionally, until slightly thickened, about 2 minutes.

Serve the sauce over the chops. Makes 4 servings.

* Brands may vary by region; substitute a similar product.

Entrées

Roasted Garlic Prime Rib Roast with Fennel
Kirkland Signature/Tyson

2 fennel bulbs

4 medium carrots, peeled and cut into 1-inch chunks

1 large white onion, cut into 1-inch chunks

1 tablespoon olive oil

1 Kirkland Signature prime rib beef roast, 3 1/2-4 pounds

Salt and black pepper

2 tablespoons whole fennel seeds, toasted

1/4 cup prepared roasted garlic puree

2 cups beef broth

Preheat oven to 350°F.

Remove tops of fennel bulbs and reserve. Cut the bulbs into 1 1/2-inch chunks. Combine with carrots and onions in a roasting pan. Toss with olive oil.

Season the roast with salt and pepper to taste.

In a small bowl, combine toasted fennel seeds with roasted garlic puree. Spread the mixture over the top of the roast. Place the roast on top of the vegetables.

Cook, covered, for 1 1/2 hours. Uncover and cook until desired doneness is reached. Remove beef to a carving board and let it rest for 20 minutes before carving.

Thirty minutes before the roast is done, prepare the fennel sauce: Cut reserved fennel bulb tops into 1 1/2-inch pieces. Combine with beef broth in a small saucepan. Simmer for 30 minutes. Strain. Serve the sauce with the roast. Makes 4 servings.

Sunday Dinner Pot Roast
McCormick

3 pounds boneless beef chuck roast (about 2 inches thick)

2 teaspoons McCormick* Grill Mates Montreal Steak Seasoning

1 cup beef broth

1/2 teaspoon dried basil leaves

1/4 teaspoon dried oregano leaves

1/4 teaspoon dried thyme leaves

4 small potatoes, peeled and halved

4 carrots, cut into 1-inch pieces

1 medium onion, cut into wedges

Flour for thickening (optional)

Preheat oven to 350°F.

Place roast in a 3-quart baking dish. Sprinkle with steak seasoning.

Mix beef broth, basil, oregano and thyme; pour over the meat. Cover.

Bake for 1 1/2 hours.

Place potatoes, carrots and onion in the pan around the roast. Cover and bake for 1 1/2 hours longer, or until the roast is tender.

Slice the roast across the grain. Arrange on a serving platter with the vegetables. If desired, thicken pan juices with flour before serving. Makes 8 servings.

Brands may vary by region; substitute a similar product.

Montreal Peppered Steak
McCormick

1/2 cup olive oil

1/4 cup soy sauce

4 teaspoons McCormick* Grill Mates Montreal Steak Seasoning

2 pounds boneless beef sirloin or New York strip steaks

GARLIC MASHED NEW POTATOES

2 pounds small red potatoes

1/2 cup grated Parmesan cheese

1 1/4 teaspoons McCormick* Grill Mates Montreal Steak Seasoning

1 teaspoon garlic powder

1 cup milk

1/2 cup sour cream

2 tablespoons butter

Mix olive oil, soy sauce and steak seasoning in a small bowl.

Place steaks in a large resealable plastic bag or a glass dish. Add marinade; turn to coat well. Refrigerate for 30 minutes, or longer for extra flavor.

Remove steaks from the marinade. Discard any remaining marinade.

Grill steaks over medium-high heat for 6-8 minutes per side, or until cooked to taste.

To prepare the potatoes, cut in quarters and place in a medium saucepan. Cover with cold water. Bring to a boil, reduce heat to medium and cook for 10 minutes, or until potatoes are fork-tender. Drain and return to the saucepan on low heat.

Sprinkle potatoes with Parmesan, steak seasoning and garlic powder. Mash potatoes, gradually adding milk, sour cream and butter. Mix until potatoes are fluffy. Serve immediately. Makes 8 servings.

Brands may vary by region; substitute a similar product.

Beef Sirloin and Portobello Stew
Horizon International

4 Kirkland Signature frozen sirloin patties, thawed

1/3 cup all-purpose flour

1 tablespoon extra-virgin olive oil

6 cups chopped portobello mushroom caps

2 cups frozen pearl onions

2 plum tomatoes

2 cups frozen cut green beans

1 14-ounce can reduced-sodium beef broth

2/3 cup red wine

2 teaspoons chopped fresh thyme or 1/2 teaspoon dried

1/2 teaspoon salt

1/4 teaspoon freshly ground pepper

Place sirloin patties in a bowl and sprinkle with flour.

Heat oil in a large saucepan over medium-high heat. Add patties (reserving excess flour) and cook until browned. Remove from the pan.

Add mushrooms, onions and tomatoes to the pan and cook, scraping up any browned bits, until the vegetables have released their juices, about 3 minutes. Sprinkle the reserved flour over the vegetables; stir to coat. Add green beans, beef broth, wine, thyme, salt and pepper; increase heat to a boil, stirring often. Reduce heat and simmer, stirring often, until the broth has thickened, about 5 minutes.

Cut the sirloin patties into bite-size pieces and add to the pan with any accumulated juices. Cook, stirring often, until heated through, about 2 minutes. Makes 4 servings.

Citrus-Marinated Flank Steak
Paramount Citrus

1 flank steak
1 tablespoon chili powder
Salt and pepper
Grated peel and juice of
   1 Paramount Citrus* lemon

Grated peel and juice of
   2 Paramount Citrus* oranges
2-3 garlic cloves, minced
2-3 tablespoons minced
   fresh cilantro

Place steak in a bowl or a large ziplock plastic bag and season both sides with chili powder and salt and pepper to taste. Add lemon and orange peel and juice, garlic and cilantro. Marinate in the refrigerator for at least 4 hours or overnight.

Grill or pan-sear the steak.

To serve, slice the steak on the bias. This goes well with fajitas or with rice pilaf and corn. Makes 4 servings.

Brands may vary by region; substitute a similar product.

PARAMOUNT CITRUS

Spicy Lime Steaks with Cheesy Chili Lime Potato Wedges
Market Source

STEAKS
Juice of 1 Market Source* lime
1 teaspoon garlic powder
1 teaspoon ground coriander
1 teaspoon ground cumin
1 teaspoon salt
1 teaspoon freshly ground pepper
2 8-ounce eye of round steaks

POTATO WEDGES
Nonstick cooking spray
2 teaspoons grated Market Source* lime peel
2 tablespoons Market Source* lime juice
2 tablespoons extra-virgin olive oil
1/4 teaspoon garlic powder
1/4 teaspoon chili powder
1/2 teaspoon onion powder
4 large Yukon Gold potatoes
Salt and pepper
1/4 cup grated Cheddar Jack cheese

To prepare the steaks, combine lime juice, garlic powder, coriander, cumin, salt and pepper in a large zippered bag. Add steaks and coat well. Refrigerate for at least 30 minutes.

Grill or broil the steaks for 5 minutes on each side, or until cooked to taste.

To prepare the potatoes, preheat oven to 425°F. Coat a baking sheet with cooking spray.

Combine grated lime peel and juice, olive oil, and garlic, chili and onion powders in a large zippered bag. Mix well.

Clean and cut potatoes into 1/2-inch-thick wedges and add to the bag. Seal and toss to coat thoroughly.

Place potato wedges on the baking sheet and sprinkle with salt and pepper to taste. Bake for 25 minutes.

Remove from the oven and sprinkle with cheese. Return to the oven and continue baking for an additional 10 minutes, or until the potatoes are tender and the cheese is golden brown. Makes 2 servings.

Brands may vary by region; substitute a similar product.

Beef Fajita Burgers
Dakota Beef

1 ⅓ pounds Dakota Beef* organic ground beef
3 tablespoons Worcestershire sauce
1 ¼ tablespoons chili powder
1 ¼ teaspoons ground cumin
2 tablespoons fresh thyme
Hot sauce to taste
¾ tablespoon grill seasoning
4 crusty rolls

PEPPERS AND ONIONS
1 tablespoon olive oil
2 red bell peppers, seeded and sliced
1 yellow onion, sliced
1 jalapeño chile, seeded and chopped
2 cups green salsa

In a bowl, combine beef, Worcestershire sauce, chili powder, cumin, thyme, hot sauce and grill seasoning; mix well. Form into 4 patties.

Grill burgers to desired doneness.

To prepare the peppers and onions, heat olive oil in a sauté pan over medium heat. Add bell peppers, onions and jalapeño; sauté until tender. Stir in salsa and heat just until warmed.

Place burgers on rolls and top with peppers and onions. Makes 4 servings.

Brands may vary by region; substitute a similar product.

Steak Sandwiches with Horseradish Mayo
La Brea Bakery

1 1-pound piece flank steak
Kosher salt
Freshly cracked black pepper
4 tablespoons butter, divided
3 medium onions, thinly sliced
1 1/2 tablespoons minced shallots
8 ounces large fresh shiitake
   mushrooms, stemmed,
   caps thinly sliced
4 La Brea Bakery* French
   Demi Baguettes

HORSERADISH MAYO
1/2 cup mayonnaise
1/4 cup prepared white horseradish
Kosher salt
Freshly cracked black pepper

To prepare the horseradish mayo, combine mayonnaise and horseradish in a small bowl. Season to taste with salt and pepper.

Pat steak dry and season both sides well with salt and pepper.

Melt 1 tablespoon butter in a large heavy skillet over medium-high heat. Add steak to the skillet and cook for about 5 minutes on each side. Transfer the meat to a cutting board and let stand for 5 minutes.

In the same skillet, melt 3 tablespoons butter over medium-high heat. Add onions and shallots; sauté until golden brown. Add mushrooms and sauté until tender, about 5 minutes. Season to taste with salt and pepper.

Slice demi baguettes in half. Generously spread horseradish mayo on both sides. Thinly slice the steak against the grain and divide among the rolls. Top with the onion and mushroom mixture. Cover the sandwiches with the top half of the baguettes. Makes 4 servings.

* Brands may vary by region; substitute a similar product.

Mini Meatloaf Burgers
Lea & Perrins

1/4 cup Lea & Perrins* Worcestershire sauce

2 tablespoons Heinz* tomato ketchup

1 pound lean ground beef

1/4 cup finely chopped onions or shallots

Salt and pepper (optional)

Sliced cheese

Sliced tomatoes

Rolls

In a medium bowl, combine Worcestershire sauce, ketchup, ground beef, onions, and salt and pepper to taste. Shape into 4 patties.

In a large skillet, cook burgers over medium-high heat for 5-7 minutes on each side, or until cooked through.

Serve with sliced cheese, tomatoes and rolls. Makes 4 servings.

Tip: Be sure to shake well before measuring out the Worcestershire sauce.

Brands may vary by region; substitute a similar product.

Sweet Glazed Pork Roast with Pistachios
Kirkland Signature/Paramount Farms

2–2 1/2-pound boneless pork loin, trimmed and tied

24 whole Kirkland Signature pistachio kernels

4-5 large garlic cloves, cut into 24 pieces

HONEY GLAZE

2 tablespoons honey

2 tablespoons dry sherry

1 teaspoon fresh rosemary

1/8 teaspoon ground cinnamon

1/8 teaspoon ground pepper

SHERRY SAUCE

1 tablespoon honey

3 tablespoons dry sherry

1/4 teaspoon fresh rosemary

Preheat oven to 325°F.

With a sharp knife, make 24 slits, 1 inch deep, over entire pork roast. Insert 1 pistachio kernel and 1 piece of garlic into each slit.

Roast for 1 1/2-2 hours, or until the internal temperature is 155°F.

To prepare the glaze, combine all ingredients in a small bowl and mix well. Baste pork with the glaze several times during roasting.

Transfer the roast to a serving platter; cover with foil and let stand for 20 minutes.

To prepare the sauce, combine all ingredients in a small saucepan. Cook over medium heat for 1 minute.

Top pork with sauce and serve immediately. Makes 6-8 servings.

Cider-Glazed Ham with Fuji Apples
Yakima Fresh

1 10-pound cook-before-you-eat ham
3 cups nonalcoholic sparkling cider, divided
1 tablespoon Dijon mustard
1 cup packed brown sugar
20 cloves

APPLES

8-10 (about 4 pounds) small Yakima Fresh* Fuji apples
1/2 cup golden raisins
1/2 cup packed brown sugar

SAUCE

1/4 cup brandy
3 tablespoons golden raisins
1/2 teaspoon grated nutmeg
1/2 teaspoon ground cloves

Preheat oven to 350°F.

Place ham in a roasting pan; pour half of cider over it. Bake for 3-3 1/2 hours, or until internal temperature is 170°F. Pour additional cider over ham every 30 minutes. Remove ham from the oven and let cool slightly; carve off visible fat.

Combine mustard and brown sugar; spread over ham. Push cloves into meat evenly. Return ham to the pan.

To prepare the apples, score in a horizontal circle with a knife to prevent bursting. Remove core from apples. Cut off end of each core and replace in the bottom of apples. Combine raisins and sugar; stuff into apples. Arrange apples around the ham.

Increase oven temperature to 400°F. Bake until ham's surface is glazed, about 30 minutes, basting with pan juices every 10 minutes, adding more cider if necessary. Transfer to a board and carve.

To prepare the sauce, pour drippings into a saucepan; skim off grease. Add brandy and whisk while bringing to a boil. If sauce is too thick, add cider. Add raisins and simmer for 2 minutes. Whisk in nutmeg and cloves. Transfer to a sauceboat for serving. Makes 8-10 servings.

Brands may vary by region; substitute a similar product.

Mediterranean Dried Plum and Olive Chicken
Kirkland Signature/Sunsweet

2 garlic cloves, minced

2/3 cup Sunsweet pitted dried plums, chopped

1/3 cup small green pitted olives

2 tablespoons capers, with liquid

1/4 cup marinated bell peppers

2 tablespoons olive oil

2 tablespoons white wine vinegar

1 tablespoon dried oregano

1/8 teaspoon salt

1/8 teaspoon ground pepper

4 boneless, skinless chicken breast fillets (approx. 2 pounds)

1/4 cup packed brown sugar

1/3 cup dry white wine

In a bowl, combine garlic, dried plums, olives, capers, bell peppers, olive oil, vinegar, oregano, salt and pepper. Mix well.

Place chicken breasts in a 15-by-10-inch baking dish. Spoon the dried-plum mixture evenly over the chicken. Marinate in the refrigerator for 15 minutes, or up to 8 hours.

Preheat oven to 350°F.

Sprinkle brown sugar over the chicken and then pour in wine.

Bake for 1 hour, spooning juices over the chicken several times while baking.

Transfer the chicken to a platter, pouring sauce over the top. Makes 4-6 servings.

Oven-Roasted Tuscan-Style Chicken with Fingerling Potatoes
Kirkland Signature/Tyson

4 Kirkland Signature/ Tyson* boneless, skinless chicken breasts

1 tablespoon canola oil

1 tablespoon Tuscan seasoning (see note)

1 medium white onion, cut in 1/4-inch dice

4 garlic cloves, thinly sliced

1 red bell pepper, seeded and cut in 1/4-inch dice

1 pound fingerling potatoes, halved lengthwise

1/4 cup white wine

1 14 1/2-ounce can stewed tomatoes

2 tablespoons thinly sliced fresh basil

4 slices fresh mozzarella

Preheat oven to 350°F.

Place chicken in a mixing bowl. Add oil and Tuscan seasoning. Turn to coat. Set aside.

Heat a heavy, oven-safe saucepan over medium heat. Add chicken to the pan. Cook for 3-4 minutes, or until browned. Turn chicken over and brown the other side.

Add onion, garlic, bell pepper and potatoes to the pan. Cook for 2 minutes. Add wine and tomatoes.

Place the pan in the oven. Cook, uncovered, for 20-25 minutes, or until the internal temperature of the chicken is 165°F.

Stir basil into the sauce in the pan. Place cheese on top of the chicken. Return the pan to the oven until the cheese melts. Sprinkle additional Tuscan seasoning on cheese, if desired. Makes 4 servings.

Note: Tuscan seasoning is a bold, spicy Italian blend of oregano, paprika, fennel, garlic, onion and other ingredients.

Brands may vary by region; substitute a similar product.

Asian Grilled Chicken
Yoshida

6 boneless chicken breast halves

2 cups Mr. Yoshida's* Original Gourmet Sauce

Toasted sesame seeds, for garnish (optional)

Orange slices, for garnish (optional)

Place chicken breasts in a nonreactive dish and pour Gourmet Sauce over them to coat well. Cover the dish with plastic wrap and marinate in the refrigerator for 2-4 hours.

Preheat grill to medium heat.

Remove chicken from the marinade; discard the marinade. Grill chicken until thoroughly cooked, brushing with additional Gourmet Sauce.

Transfer the chicken to a platter and sprinkle with toasted sesame seeds. Garnish the platter with orange slices. Serve immediately. Makes 6 servings.

* Brands may vary by region; substitute a similar product.

Mandarin Braised Chicken
Festival

2 tablespoons olive oil

8 each chicken legs and thighs

1 large onion, diced

2 large carrots, diced

1 celery stalk, diced

4 garlic cloves, sliced

1 tablespoon cracked coriander seed

1/2 teaspoon red pepper flakes

3 11-ounce cans Festival* mandarin oranges

1 1/2 cups white wine

1/2 cup cider vinegar

Chicken stock to cover, about 2 cups

1/2 cup cold butter

Steamed rice

1/4 cup fresh cilantro, coarsely chopped

Preheat oven to 275°F.

Heat olive oil in a heavy-bottomed ovenproof pan over medium-high heat. Sear chicken, half at a time, on both sides until golden brown. Reduce heat if the pan begins to darken.

Remove chicken and add onion, carrots, celery, garlic, coriander and red pepper flakes to the pan; sauté until onion is golden.

Lower the heat to medium and add mandarin orange juice, wine and vinegar. Reduce the liquid until almost gone.

Return chicken to the pan and add stock to cover. Bring to a simmer, cover and bake for approximately 2 hours, or until fork tender.

Remove chicken and strain the liquid. Add cold butter to the liquid and stir until melted. Add mandarin oranges.

Serve chicken and sauce over rice, garnished with cilantro. Makes 8 servings.

Recipe courtesy of Chef Tyler Hefford-Anderson.
* Brands may vary by region; substitute a similar product.

Grilled Chicken with Ancho Chile Sauce
Mazola Oils

SPICE BLEND
2 tablespoons brown sugar
3 tablespoons ancho chile powder
1 1/2 tablespoons smoked paprika
1 tablespoon ground cumin
1 1/2 teaspoons garlic powder
1/2 teaspoon salt
1/8 teaspoon ground cloves

CHICKEN
1/4 cup Mazola* corn oil
1/4 cup water
4 boneless, skinless chicken breast halves

ANCHO CHILE SAUCE
2 tablespoons Mazola* corn oil
1/2 cup finely minced onion
1 8-ounce can tomato sauce
2 tablespoons dark corn syrup
1 1/2 teaspoons cocoa

To prepare the spice blend, combine all ingredients in a small bowl. Mix well.

To prepare the chicken, combine 2 tablespoons spice blend, corn oil and water in a large resealable plastic bag, blending well. Add chicken, seal the bag and turn to coat chicken thoroughly with spices. Marinate in the refrigerator a minimum of 15 minutes.

Remove chicken from the marinade; discard any remaining marinade. Grill chicken until cooked through, about 10-15 minutes (internal temperature should reach 170°F).

To prepare Ancho Chile Sauce, heat oil in a small saucepan over medium heat. Add onions and cook until softened. Add remaining spice blend (approximately 5 tablespoons), tomato sauce and corn syrup, stirring well. Heat for 1 minute, then remove from the heat. Stir in cocoa until blended. Serve immediately, or cover and refrigerate for up to 3 days.

Serve chicken with Ancho Chile Sauce. Makes 4 servings.

Brands may vary by region; substitute a similar product.

Mazola®

Chef Allen's Fruity Roasted Chicken
Chestnut Hill Farms/Legend Produce

1 cup freshly cubed
   pineapple

1 cup freshly cubed mango

1 cup freshly cubed melon

1 tablespoon whole
   cumin seed

2 garlic cloves, crushed

1 small onion, chopped

1 tablespoon kosher
   salt, divided

1 3-pound chicken

1/2 teaspoon ground
   black pepper

2 tablespoons olive oil

Preheat oven to 400°F.

In a bowl, combine pineapple, mango, melon, cumin, garlic, onion and 1 teaspoon salt.

Fill cavity of bird with fruit mix; reserve the remainder. Plump the chicken together so the legs and wings are set back toward the bird; tie the legs together. Season with salt and pepper. Rub with olive oil.

Place chicken in a roasting pan and set in the oven, then lower the heat to 350°F. Roast for 20 minutes, then add the reserved fruit to the pan. Continue roasting for another 30 minutes. Test with a skewer for doneness; juices should run clear. Makes 4 servings.

Recipe courtesy of Chef Allen Susser.

Easy Chicken Piccata with Sun-Dried Tomato Orzo
Kirkland Signature/Perdue

4 Kirkland Signature/
   Perdue* Individually
   Wrapped Frozen
   Boneless, Skinless
   Chicken Breasts

1 1/2 cups hot cooked orzo

1/2 cup chopped
   green onions

1 tablespoon olive oil

1/4 cup chopped
   sun-dried tomato

1/2 cup chicken broth,
   divided

2 tablespoons lemon juice

2 tablespoons
   capers, drained

2 tablespoons butter

1/4 cup chopped
   fresh parsley

Lemon slices, for garnish

Cook frozen chicken in a large skillet according to package directions.

While chicken is cooking, prepare orzo according to package directions.

In a separate skillet, sauté green onions in olive oil over medium heat for 1 minute. Add sun-dried tomato and 1/8-1/4 cup of the chicken broth. Add hot cooked orzo, stirring to combine. Set aside and keep warm.

When the chicken is done, remove and place on a platter; cover and keep warm.

To the chicken skillet add 1/4 cup chicken broth, lemon juice and capers; simmer for 2 minutes, stirring and scraping the bottom of the pan. Add butter in small amounts, stirring with each addition until melted and well combined. Stir in parsley.

Spoon the broth mixture over the chicken. Serve with the orzo and garnish with lemon slices. Makes 4 servings.

* Brands may vary by region; substitute a similar product.

Marinated Grilled Salmon with Sautéed Oranges
Sunkist Growers

4 fresh salmon steaks,
   about 4-6 ounces each
Cooking spray
1 garlic clove, minced
2 tablespoons chopped
   cilantro leaves

Zest and juice of 1 Sunkist* orange
1 tablespoon plus 2 teaspoons
   toasted sesame oil, divided
2 Sunkist* oranges, peeled, cut in
   4 horizontal slices each
Sesame seeds (optional)

Pat salmon steaks dry with paper towels. Coat a shallow baking dish with cooking spray and place salmon steaks in the pan.

Combine garlic, cilantro, orange zest and juice, and 1 tablespoon sesame oil in a bowl. Reserve 1/4 cup marinade for grilling. Pour remaining mixture over salmon. Place in the refrigerator and let marinate for 30 minutes.

Prepare grill at medium-high heat. (Use a grilling basket if possible.) Remove salmon from the marinade and grill, basting with reserved marinade, until the fish flakes easily, about 4-6 minutes on each side. Transfer salmon to a plate; cover to keep warm.

In a nonstick skillet, heat remaining 2 teaspoons sesame oil over medium heat. Place orange slices in the pan and cook until just warmed, only about 1 minute on each side. (Cooking longer will cause slices to fall apart.)

To serve, top each salmon steak with two sautéed orange slices and sprinkle with sesame seeds. Makes 4 servings.

Tip: Use Sunkist Navel, Valencia or Cara Cara oranges.

* Brands may vary by region; substitute a similar product.

Sunkist

Asian-Inspired Alaska Wild Salmon with Wasabi Mashed Potatoes
Alaska Glacier Seafood

2-3 pounds Alaska Glacier Seafood* wild salmon fillet (sockeye, king or coho), skin on

¹/₂ cup olive oil

¹/₂ cup soy sauce

¹/₂ cup brown sugar

4-5 medium potatoes

Salt

2 tablespoons butter

¹/₂ cup sour cream

1 tablespoon wasabi oil, paste or powder, or to taste

Cut salmon into 2- to 3-inch-wide pieces, leaving the skin on.

Combine olive oil, soy sauce and brown sugar in a glass bowl, mixing until well blended.

Place salmon in a sealable plastic bag and pour marinade on top. Seal the bag and marinate salmon pieces for 1 ¹/₂-2 hours, rotating every 30 minutes.

Grill salmon at a medium temperature with skin side up for 5-7 minutes, then rotate pieces with skin side down and cook an additional 5-7 minutes, or until the meat can be flaked apart.

Meanwhile, wash, peel and dice potatoes. Boil in salted water until tender; drain. Whip potatoes with butter, sour cream, dash of salt and wasabi oil, paste or powder. Makes 4-6 servings.

* Brands may vary by region; substitute a similar product.

Stuffed Salmon Fillets in Parchment with Spinach
Okami

2 tablespoons butter, softened

2 15-by-15-inch squares parchment paper

4 cups cleaned fresh spinach

Salt and pepper

2 portions Kirkland Signature stuffed salmon entrée

Chopped fresh parsley

Preheat oven to 400°F. Spread butter on half of each sheet of parchment paper.

Place 2 cups of spinach over each buttered half of parchment paper. Sprinkle with salt and pepper to taste.

Place salmon on the spinach. Sprinkle with parsley.

Fold the parchment paper over the filling, folding and crimping the edges tightly to seal and enclose completely.

Place on a baking sheet and bake for 25 minutes. Set the packets on plates and serve. Makes 2 servings.

Grilled Salmon with Brown Sugar Glaze
Smoki Foods

4 6-ounce Smoki Foods* Atlantic or
   sockeye salmon portions

1 tablespoon seasoning salt
   (Johnny's or McCormick
   Montreal Chicken Seasoning
   are both good)

$1/2$ tablespoon garlic powder

$1/2$ cup packed brown sugar

Preheat grill to medium heat.

Place salmon portions, evenly spaced, on a sheet of foil. Roll up the edges of the foil (brown sugar is a good fire-starter).

Sprinkle seasoning salt and garlic powder evenly over salmon.

Spread brown sugar over seasoned salmon by hand, coating completely with about $1/8$ inch of sugar.

Grill salmon for 8-10 minutes, or until it flakes easily with a fork. It is not necessary to turn the fillets if they are grilled slowly. Makes 4 servings.

* Brands may vary by region; substitute a similar product.

Smoki Foods

"In a Heartbeat" Atlantic Salmon with Red Curry-Coconut Sauce
Camanchaca

1 13 ½-ounce can coconut milk

1 cup tomato basil sauce

1 teaspoon grated fresh ginger

¾ cube shrimp-flavor bouillon

¼-1 teaspoon red curry paste

½ bunch fresh cilantro, chopped

Salt and pepper

4 6- to 8-ounce Camanchaca* salmon fillets

Vegetable oil

Cooked rice

In a medium saucepan, combine coconut milk, tomato sauce, ginger, shrimp bouillon and curry paste to taste. Bring sauce to a quick boil over medium-high heat, stirring constantly; immediately lower temperature to medium-low and simmer for 7 minutes, stirring occasionally. Stir in cilantro and remove from the heat. Season to taste with salt and pepper.

Meanwhile, brush salmon with vegetable oil and season to taste with salt and pepper on both sides. Grill for 3-5 minutes on each side, or until cooked to taste.

Pour the sauce over the salmon and serve with rice. Makes 4 servings.

Tip: This goes well with stir-fried carrots, snow peas, red bell peppers and bamboo shoots.

Recipe courtesy of Camanchaca Chef Jorge Cebreros.
* Brands may vary by region; substitute a similar product.

Dilled Salmon Cakes
Quaker

SAUCE

½ cup plain nonfat yogurt

⅓ cup seeded, chopped tomato

⅓ cup seeded, chopped cucumber

1 tablespoon finely chopped onion

1 tablespoon finely chopped fresh dill or 1 teaspoon dried dill weed

SALMON CAKES

1 14 ¾-ounce can pink salmon, drained, skin and bones removed

¾ cup Quaker Oats (quick or old-fashioned, uncooked)

⅓ cup fat-free milk

2 egg whites, lightly beaten

2 tablespoons finely chopped onion

1 tablespoon finely chopped fresh dill or 1 teaspoon dried dill weed

¼ teaspoon salt (optional)

Nonstick cooking spray

To prepare the sauce, combine all ingredients in a small bowl; mix well. Cover and chill while making the salmon cakes.

To prepare the salmon cakes, combine salmon, oats, milk, egg whites, onion, dill and salt in a medium bowl; mix well. Let stand for 5 minutes. Shape into 5 oval patties about 1 inch thick.

Lightly spray a nonstick skillet with cooking spray. Cook salmon cakes over medium heat for 3-4 minutes on each side, or until golden brown and heated through. Serve with the sauce. Makes 5 servings.

Grilled Salmon Fillet with Summer Vegetable Relish
Pacific Seafood Group

1 cucumber, peeled, seeds removed, diced

1 tomato, diced

1/4 red onion, diced

1 cup fresh corn kernels, blanched, or frozen corn

1 zucchini, diced

1 tablespoon chopped fresh dill

1 tablespoon sherry vinegar

1/4 cup olive oil, divided

Salt and pepper

4 6-ounce pieces salmon fillet

In a bowl, combine vegetables, dill, vinegar, 3 tablespoons olive oil, and salt and pepper to taste. Let rest for at least 30 minutes.

Meanwhile, season salmon with salt and pepper to taste. Brush with the remaining olive oil. Grill over medium-high heat about 5-7 minutes per side, or until the fish flakes easily.

When the fish is done, place on plates and garnish with Summer Vegetable Relish. Makes 4 servings.

PacificSeafood™

Honey Mustard Salmon
Hellmann's/Best Foods

1/2 cup Hellmann's or Best Foods Real Mayonnaise

2 tablespoons Hellmann's Deli Mustard

2 green onions, chopped, plus more for garnish

1 tablespoon honey

1 teaspoon apple cider vinegar

1/8 teaspoon ground black pepper

Pinch of salt

4 salmon fillets or steaks (about 1 pound)

In a medium bowl, combine mayonnaise, mustard, 2 chopped green onions, honey, vinegar, pepper and salt. Reserve 1/3 of mayonnaise mixture.

Grill or broil salmon, brushing with remaining mayonnaise mixture, turning once, until salmon flakes easily with a fork.

Serve salmon with the reserved mayonnaise mixture and garnish, if desired, with additional chopped green onions. Makes 4 servings.

Patricia's Salmon Basilico Pomodoro
Kirkland Signature/Marine Harvest

6 Kirkland Signature frozen salmon portions
1 bunch fresh basil

1 cup chopped fresh tomatoes
2 tablespoons olive oil
Salt and pepper

Thaw salmon, removing from the vacuum bag or puncturing the bag.

Preheat oven to 375°F.

Reserve a few basil leaves for garnish; chop the remaining leaves. Mix chopped basil with tomatoes and olive oil in a bowl.

Place thawed salmon portions in a baking dish. Cover with some of the tomato-basil mixture, reserving the remainder for later use. Season to taste with salt and pepper.

Bake for 15-20 minutes, or until the salmon is cooked to taste.

Garnish with basil leaves and the reserved tomato-basil mixture. Serve with rice, mashed potatoes or your favorite vegetable. Makes 6 servings.

Minted Salmon and Asparagus Stir-Fry
AquaGold Seafood

2 tablespoons Asian fish sauce*

2 tablespoons oyster sauce*

2 tablespoons cold water

2 teaspoons brown sugar

1 fresh red chile, seeded and minced

2 tablespoons olive oil

1 1/2 pounds skinless, boneless fresh Atlantic salmon, cut into 4 pieces

2 garlic cloves, minced

1 bunch thin asparagus, cut into 1-inch pieces

1/2 cup chopped fresh mint

In a small bowl, whisk together fish sauce, oyster sauce, water, sugar and chile; set aside.

Heat olive oil over medium-high heat in a wok or large skillet. Place salmon in the hot oil and sprinkle with garlic. Cook for 1 minute, turn and cook for 2 more minutes.

Add asparagus and reserved sauce mixture. Bring to a boil, cover, reduce heat to medium and simmer for 3-5 minutes, or until the salmon just flakes and the asparagus is crisp-tender.

Stir in mint and serve. Makes 4 servings.

*Available at Asian markets and in the Asian food section of most large supermarkets.

Baked Salmon Fillets with Simple Cream Sauce
Multiexport Foods

6 5- to 6-ounce salmon fillets

1/2 teaspoon salt

1/2 teaspoon pepper

1 10 1/2-ounce can cream of celery soup

1/2 cup reduced-fat milk

2 tablespoons Dijon mustard

2 tablespoons butter, melted

1 cup dry bread crumbs

Preheat oven to 350°F. Lightly grease a baking pan that will hold fish in a single layer.

Place salmon in the pan. Sprinkle with salt and pepper.

In a bowl, blend soup, milk, mustard and butter. Pour over the fillets. Sprinkle with bread crumbs.

Bake for 35 minutes, or until the fish flakes. Makes 6 servings.

Multiexport Foods

Killer Salmon
Monster Energy

2 cans Monster* energy drink (green label)

8 ounces jumbo lump crabmeat

2 ounces spinach leaves, cut into long strips

4 6-ounce Tasmanian salmon fillets

Salt and pepper

Freshly chopped parsley

2 tablespoons unsalted butter, cut into pats

Preheat oven to 400°F.

Pour Monster into a saucepan and bring to a boil. Simmer until reduced to one-third. Let cool.

Combine crabmeat and spinach in a bowl. Coat with some of the reduced Monster mixture. Set aside.

Lay salmon skin side up and make a cut width-wise. Open each side of the salmon fillet. Sprinkle with salt and pepper to taste.

Put crabmeat mixture in the center of each salmon fillet. Close the halves and flip over in a lightly oiled baking pan.

Cut across so that a little of the crabmeat is visible. Drizzle some of the Monster mixture over the salmon. Sprinkle with salt, pepper and fresh parsley to taste. Cover with foil.

Cook for 20-25 minutes, removing the foil during the final 5 minutes. Remove from the oven and let cool slightly.

Warm remainder of the Monster reduction. Whisking well, add butter, salt and pepper. Spoon the sauce over the salmon. Makes 4 servings.

Created by Chef Tara Kazimir of Michele's Restaurant at Dover Downs Hotel & Casino, Delaware.
* Brands may vary by region; substitute a similar product.

Salmon Ravioli
Orval Kent Foods

2 pieces Kirkland Signature stuffed salmon entrée (1/2 package)

1 tablespoon minced chives

2 tablespoons heavy cream

Salt and black pepper

1 egg, beaten

1 tablespoon water

1 package 3-inch-square wonton wrappers

1 tablespoon butter, softened

Chopped tomatoes, for garnish

Lemon wedges, for garnish

Separate the stuffing from the salmon. Dice salmon into small pieces, about 3/8 inch.

In a bowl, combine diced salmon, stuffing, chives, heavy cream, and salt and pepper to taste.

In a separate bowl, mix egg with water.

On a clean surface or cutting board, lay out half of the wonton wrappers. Brush 1/4 inch of egg wash around the edges of each square.

Place 1/2-1 tablespoon of the salmon mixture in the center of each wonton wrapper, pressing down gently and leaving the wrapper edges exposed. Top with remaining wonton wrappers and press to firmly seal the edges.

Place the ravioli in a pot of boiling water and cook for 5-7 minutes, or until tender.

Remove ravioli from the water and place in a bowl. Add softened butter and toss to coat.

Garnish with chopped tomatoes and lemon wedges. Serve immediately. Makes 4-5 servings.

Roasted Apple and Salmon Salad
Pennsylvania Apple/New York Apple

1 5-ounce piece salmon fillet with skin

2 teaspoons extra-virgin olive oil, divided, plus more for drizzling

Salt and pepper

1 Eastern Empire* apple, cored and peeled, cut in 6 pieces

1/2 tablespoon chopped fresh chives

2 cups salad greens

2 tablespoons pumpkin seeds, lightly toasted

DRESSING

1/4 cup red wine vinegar

3 tablespoons water

1/2 cup extra-virgin olive oil

1/2 1-ounce packet Italian salad dressing mix

Preheat oven to 425°F.

Rub salmon all over with 1 teaspoon oil and season to taste with salt and pepper. Roast, skin side down, on a foil-lined baking sheet in upper third of oven until fish is just cooked through, about 12 minutes.

At the same time, drizzle apple with 1 teaspoon olive oil and roast until tender, about 12 minutes.

To prepare the dressing, whisk together all ingredients until combined.

Cut salmon in half crosswise, lift flesh from skin with a metal spatula and transfer to a plate. Discard skin, drizzle salmon with oil and sprinkle with chives.

Arrange salad greens on plates and top with pumpkin seeds, apples and salmon.

Drizzle with dressing to taste. Makes 2 servings.

Tip: Other Eastern apple varieties such as Jonagold or Gingergold are also good choices.

* Brands may vary by region; substitute a similar product.

Grilled Shrimp and Mango Salad
Freska Produce

3 tablespoons thinly sliced green onions

1/3 cup lime juice

2 tablespoons fish sauce (sold in Asian markets)

1 teaspoon sugar

1 small garlic clove, minced

1 small hot chile, such as serrano, seeded and minced

2 large, firm Freska* mangoes, peeled and shredded

1 pound shrimp (25-30 per pound)

8 slender skewers

2 cups salad greens

Lime slices, for garnish (optional)

Combine green onions, lime juice, fish sauce, sugar, garlic and chile in a bowl. Mix in shredded mango. Chill while preparing shrimp.

Shell and devein shrimp and rinse well; divide into 4 portions. Thread 1 portion onto a skewer. Run a second skewer through the shrimp 1/2 to 1 inch from the first skewer, to keep them flat. Repeat with remaining shrimp.

Grill shrimp on a medium-hot grill, covered, for about 3 minutes on each side, or until opaque but still a bit moist in the center of the thickest parts.

Place greens on a platter. Mound the mango mixture on the greens, using a slotted spoon. Place shrimp over the mango salad and garnish with lime slices. Makes 4 servings.

* Brands may vary by region; substitute a similar product.

Prawn Kebabs with Gold Pineapple and Lime Marinade
The Oppenheimer Group

MARINADE

1/4 cup lime juice

1/4 cup dry sherry

1/4 cup olive oil

3 tablespoons soy sauce

3 tablespoons honey

1/4 cup chopped fresh cilantro

2 garlic cloves, minced

1 tablespoon grated fresh ginger

1 tablespoon Dijon mustard

1/2 teaspoon red pepper flakes

KEBABS

1 1/2 pounds raw prawns, peeled

10 bamboo skewers, soaked in water

1 large red onion, peeled, sliced into 1 1/2-inch pieces

1 large Oppenheimer* red, yellow or orange sweet bell pepper, seeded and cut into 1 1/2-inch pieces

1 fresh, gold-fleshed Oppenheimer*pineapple, peeled, cored and sliced into 3/4-inch-thick wedges

To prepare the marinade, combine all ingredients in a small bowl and whisk to blend.

Pour 2/3 cup marinade over the prawns; refrigerate for 30 minutes.

Assemble the kebabs, starting with a piece of onion, and alternate with the prawns, bell pepper and pineapple, leaving 1/2 inch of skewer showing at either end.

Grill the kebabs on medium-high heat, basting with the reserved marinade, until the prawns are opaque and fully cooked, about 5 minutes per side.

Serve immediately with a side dish of wild rice or garlic mashed potatoes. Makes 5 servings.

Brands may vary by region; substitute a similar product.

expect the world from us™

Chipotle Shrimp and Pineapple Kabobs
Dole

1 cup bottled Baja chipotle marinade, divided

1 1/2 pounds large shrimp, peeled and deveined

1 20-ounce can Dole* Pineapple Chunks, drained

1 medium red onion, cut into chunks

2 red *or* green bell peppers, cut into chunks

Pour 3/4 cup marinade over shrimp in a large sealable plastic bag. Refrigerate and marinate for 30 minutes.

Remove shrimp from the plastic bag and discard marinade.

Thread shrimp, pineapple chunks, onion and bell peppers onto skewers.

Grill or broil for 8 minutes, or until the shrimp turn pink, turning and brushing with reserved marinade. Discard any remaining marinade. Makes 4-6 servings.

Brands may vary by region; substitute a similar product.

Croissant Crab Salad Sandwich with Tangerine Mixed Baby Greens Salad
Kirkland Signature/Puratos

CRAB SALAD

2 cups Blue Star crab, picked over to remove shell fragments

1 cup shredded Tillamook Special Reserve Extra Sharp Cheddar

$1/2$ cup sliced green onions

2 teaspoons Kirkland Signature Herbed Seafood Rub

$3/4$ cup mayonnaise

$1/4$ cup aged-in-wood sherry

1 tablespoon fresh lemon juice

Fine sea salt and ground black pepper to taste

TANGERINE DRESSING

$1/2$ cup fresh tangerine juice

Grated peel of 1 tangerine

Juice of 1 lime

$1/8$ teaspoon sea salt

$1/4$ cup light brown sugar

2 tablespoons sliced green onions

1 tablespoon minced fresh ginger

$1/2$ cup Kirkland Signature olive oil

Freshly ground black pepper

CROISSANT CROUTONS

1 Kirkland Signature croissant, diced

1 tablespoon Kirkland Signature olive oil

1 teaspoon Kirkland Signature Herbed Seafood Rub

4 Kirkland Signature croissants

$1/4$ cup thinly sliced red onion

5 cups mixed baby greens

1 tangerine, peeled and segmented

To prepare the crab salad, place all ingredients in a bowl. Gently toss with the fingertips to combine thoroughly. Let stand for 15-30 minutes to allow flavors to blend.

To prepare the dressing, combine tangerine juice and peel, lime juice, salt, brown sugar, green onions and ginger in a bowl. Gradually whisk in olive oil until blended. Season to taste with pepper.

To prepare the croutons, preheat oven to 300°F. Toss all ingredients in a bowl. Place on a baking pan and toast for 15 minutes.

Slice open the 4 croissants. Top with crab salad.

Place red onions, mixed baby greens, tangerines and $1/2$ cup croutons in a salad bowl. Drizzle with dressing to taste and toss lightly to coat evenly. Serve within 4-5 minutes to prevent wilting. Makes 4 servings.

Northwest Grilled Garlic Dungeness Crab
Pacific Seafood Group

$1/3$ cup butter

$1/3$ cup olive oil

3 tablespoons minced garlic

Juice and grated peel of 3 lemons

4 Dungeness crabs, cleaned, cooked and cracked

Seasonal vegetables for grilling

Salt and pepper

$1/4$ cup chopped fresh parsley

$1/4$ cup chopped fresh basil

Sourdough bread

Preheat grill.

Melt butter with olive oil, garlic, and lemon juice and grated peel.

Toss crab in the butter mixture to coat. Place crab on the grill away from the flames.

Toss vegetables in the butter mixture and season to taste with salt and pepper. Place vegetables on the grill.

Cook crab for 4 minutes and turn over, brushing with the butter mixture. Turn the vegetables over. Cook until the crab is heated through and the vegetables are done. Arrange the vegetables on a platter.

Toss herbs in the remaining butter mixture. Add the crab and toss until coated. Arrange the crab on the platter. Pour the remaining butter mixture over the platter.

Serve with crusty sourdough bread. Makes 4 servings.

PacificSeafood™

Grilled Scallops with Chili-Lime Cream Sauce
Atlantic Capes Fisheries

1 ½ pounds large Atlantic Capes Fisheries sea scallops

¼ cup olive oil

Salt and pepper

¼ teaspoon red pepper flakes (optional)

2 garlic cloves, finely chopped

Cooked jasmine or white rice

CHILI-LIME CREAM SAUCE

¼ cup freshly squeezed lime juice

¼ cup white wine (not cooking wine)

1 tablespoon minced peeled fresh ginger

1 large shallot, chopped

⅓ cup heavy cream

2 tablespoons Asian sweet chili sauce or garlic chili sauce

6 tablespoons unsalted butter

Salt and pepper

Combine scallops, olive oil, salt and pepper to taste, red pepper flakes and garlic. Marinate for 30 minutes.

To prepare the sauce, combine lime juice, wine, ginger and shallot in a small saucepan. Cook over high heat until reduced by half (3 minutes). Add cream, lower heat and cook until reduced by half. Remove from the heat. Stir in chili sauce. Whisk in butter 1 piece at a time. Add salt and pepper to taste. Set aside.

Preheat barbecue grill to medium-high heat. Grill scallops until cooked to taste (don't overcook).

Serve scallops with sauce and rice. Makes 4-6 servings.

Tip: Make a bed of grilled asparagus and top with grilled scallops. Pour sauce over the scallops, or serve sauce on the side and garnish scallops with chopped parsley.

Sea Scallop Shooters Layered with Spinach and Roasted Mushrooms
American Pride Seafoods

SPINACH FILLING
1 tablespoon olive oil
1/4 cup minced red onion
1 tablespoon minced garlic
4 ounces baby spinach
1/4 cup heavy cream
1 tablespoon grated
  Parmesan cheese
1 teaspoon unseasoned dry
  bread crumbs
Salt and pepper

ROASTED MUSHROOMS
1/2 cup minced shiitake mushrooms
1/2 cup minced portobello mushrooms
1/2 cup minced crimini mushrooms
1/2 teaspoon minced garlic
1/2 tablespoon olive oil
Salt and pepper

SCALLOPS
12 American Pride Seafoods
  sea scallops
1 tablespoon sugar
1 tablespoon salt
1 tablespoon pepper
Olive oil

Preheat oven to 375°F.

To prepare the spinach filling, heat olive oil over medium heat in a sauté pan. Add onions and garlic; cook until tender. Add spinach and cook until soft. Add cream and cook until reduced by half. Lower heat and add Parmesan, bread crumbs, and salt and pepper to taste. Let cool.

To prepare the mushrooms, toss mushrooms with garlic, olive oil, and salt and pepper to taste. Roast in the oven for 15 minutes. Let cool.

To prepare the scallops, season scallops with sugar, salt and pepper. Coat a sauté pan with oil and fry scallops over medium heat until golden brown. Let cool.

Cut each scallop into thirds horizontally. Add 1 teaspoon of mushrooms to the bottom layer and 1 teaspoon of spinach filling to the middle layer. Stack spinach layer on mushroom layer and top with the third slice.

Place the assembled scallops on a baking sheet. Bake for 10-12 minutes, or until hot and bubbly. Serve immediately. Makes 4 servings.

Clams Marinière
Quality Ocean International

5 pounds Quality Ocean*
New Zealand Cockles
(littleneck clams)

1 medium onion,
finely chopped

2 garlic cloves, crushed

1/2 cup fresh parsley,
finely chopped, divided

1 bay leaf (optional)

1/2 cup dry white wine

1 tablespoon butter

Freshly ground
black pepper

1/4 cup cream

Scrub clams thoroughly and place in a large saucepan with onions, garlic, three-quarters of the parsley, and bay leaf. Add wine and butter. Grind a little black pepper on top.

Cover the pan tightly, bring to a boil over medium-high heat and steam until the clams open. Remove the clams to a warm serving dish.

Strain the clam liquid and add extra pepper to taste. Add cream and the remaining parsley. Reheat the clam sauce, but do not boil.

Pour the sauce over the clams and serve immediately as they are, or on a bed of rice or pasta. Clams being naturally salty, there is no need to add salt. Makes 4 servings.

Brands may vary by region; substitute a similar product.

QUALITY OCEAN
INTERNATIONAL

Dijon Steamed Mussels with Fennel
North Coast Seafoods

2 tablespoons butter or oil

1/2 cup diced onion

1 garlic clove, chopped

1/2 fennel bulb, sliced
very thin

1 cup white wine

2 tablespoons
Dijon mustard

1 teaspoon dried tarragon

1/4 cup heavy cream

2 pounds North Coast
Seafoods* PEI mussels

Kosher salt and pepper

Crusty bread

In a large pot, melt butter over medium heat. Add onion, garlic and fennel; sauté until soft and translucent, about 5 minutes.

Add wine, mustard and tarragon, and bring to a boil.

Add cream and mussels, cover and steam over high heat for about 5 minutes, or until the mussels have opened.

Season to taste with salt and pepper. Serve in a bowl with crusty bread. Makes 4 servings.

Brands may vary by region; substitute a similar product.

Grilled Halibut with Grilled Pineapple Salsa
Kirkland Signature

2 pounds fresh halibut fillet, cut into
   6- to 8-ounce portions
2 tablespoons olive oil
Kosher salt and freshly
   ground pepper

GRILLED PINEAPPLE SALSA
1 fresh pineapple
Kosher salt and freshly
   ground pepper

1 red onion, chopped
1 bunch fresh cilantro, chopped
1 jalapeño chile, minced (optional)
Juice of 1 lime
1-2 tablespoons olive oil
1-2 tablespoons rice vinegar

Preheat grill to high.

To prepare the salsa, stand pineapple on end and cut off the outer layer of skin. Lay pineapple on its side and cut into 1-inch-thick slices. Season with salt and pepper to taste. Place on the grill and cook for 5 minutes per side. Set aside to cool.

Cut pineapple into cubes, discarding the center core. Place in a bowl and add onion, cilantro, jalapeño, lime juice, olive oil and vinegar. Mix well. Serve at room temperature.

Brush halibut on both sides with olive oil and season to taste with salt and pepper. Place on the grill and cook for 5-6 minutes. Turn carefully and cook for another 5-6 minutes, or until it flakes easily with a fork.

Serve immediately, topped with salsa. Makes 4 servings.

Seafood and Logistics Specialist

Halibut with Jicama and Citrus Salad
Bravante Produce

JICAMA AND CITRUS SALAD

1 pound jicama, peeled and cut into $1/2$-inch cubes

1 red onion, diced

1 grapefruit, peeled

1 Bravante* orange, peeled

1 jalapeño chile, seeded and finely diced

$1/4$ cup chopped fresh cilantro

1 tablespoon freshly squeezed lime juice

3 tablespoons extra-virgin olive oil

$1/2$ teaspoon chili powder

$1/2$ teaspoon salt

6 6-ounce halibut fillets

Salt and pepper

1 ounce (2 tablespoons) butter, melted

Cilantro, for garnish

To prepare the salad, combine jicama and onion in a bowl. Cut grapefruit and orange into $1/2$-inch pieces; add to the jicama mixture. Stir in jalapeño, cilantro, lime juice and olive oil. Sprinkle with chili powder and salt. Stir well and refrigerate.

Season halibut with salt and pepper to taste. Brush with melted butter. Grill or broil the fish, being careful not to overcook it.

To serve, divide salad among 6 plates. Place halibut fillets on top of salad. Garnish with fresh cilantro. Makes 6 servings.

Tip: Substitute sea bass for halibut.

Recipe courtesy of Chef David Vartanian, The Vintage Press, Visalia, California.
* Brands may vary by region; substitute a similar product.

BRAVANTE
P R O D U C E

Lemon Garlic Alaska Halibut
American Fish & Seafood

2 tablespoons butter or olive oil

2 teaspoons minced garlic

2 4- to 6-ounce American Fish* Alaska halibut fillets

1 teaspoon lemon pepper

Pinch of salt

Fresh lemon wedges

Melt butter in a large skillet over medium-high heat. Stir in garlic.

Season halibut on both sides with lemon pepper and salt. Place halibut in the skillet and cook for 10 minutes per inch of thickness, measured at the thickest part, or until the fish flakes when tested with a fork. Flip halfway through cooking to brown on both sides.

Sprinkle halibut with lemon juice before serving. Makes 2 servings.

Tip: This recipe can be easily doubled.

* Brands may vary by region; substitute a similar product.

Barbecued Alaskan Halibut
Smoki Foods

Cooking spray
4 tablespoons butter
4 tablespoons brown sugar
4 garlic cloves, minced
2 tablespoons lemon juice

4 teaspoons soy sauce
1 teaspoon ground black pepper
4 Smoki Foods* Alaskan halibut
　　portions (approx. 6-8 ounces each)

Preheat an outdoor grill to medium-high heat, and lightly oil the grate with cooking spray.

Combine butter, brown sugar, garlic, lemon juice, soy sauce and pepper in a small saucepan. Cook over medium heat, stirring slowly, until the sugar dissolves.

Coat halibut with the sauce and place on the grill. Grill for 5 minutes on each side, basting frequently, or until the fish flakes easily with a fork. Makes 4 servings.

* Brands may vary by region; substitute a similar product.

Baked Halibut with Walnuts au Gratin
Diamond Foods

1 1/2 pounds fresh or frozen halibut fillets

Salt and pepper

Juice of 1 lemon

2 tablespoons dry white wine

1 cup finely diced toasted Diamond walnuts

1 cup grated sharp Cheddar cheese

1/4 cup milk

1/2 cup dry bread crumbs

1 tablespoon butter or margarine

Preheat oven to 400°F.

Place fish on a well-greased sheet of heavy-duty aluminum foil. Sprinkle with salt, pepper, lemon juice and wine.

Combine walnuts, grated cheese and milk; spread on top of the fish.

Sprinkle with bread crumbs and dot with butter.

Wrap the fish tightly in the foil, sealing the ends and top with double folds.

Bake for 25-30 minutes, or until the fish is tender and flaky. Makes 4 servings.

Pan-Roasted Halibut with Butternut Squash, Toasted Hazelnuts and Sage
Pacific Seafood Group

3 tablespoons butter, divided

1 butternut squash, peeled, seeded and diced

4 6-ounce halibut fillets

Salt and pepper

1 tablespoon chopped fresh sage

1 tablespoon chopped fresh chives

1 tablespoon chopped fresh parsley

1/4 onion, diced

1/2 cup white wine

1 bay leaf

1/2 cup heavy cream

1/4 teaspoon grated nutmeg

1/2 cup toasted hazelnuts

Preheat oven to 350°F.

Place a large sauté pan on medium heat. Add 2 tablespoons butter, then squash. Cover and cook for 10 minutes, stirring occasionally.

Preheat an ovenproof sauté pan over medium-high heat. Season halibut with salt and pepper. Combine herbs and coat one side of halibut with half of herbs, setting aside the rest. Melt 1 tablespoon butter in the pan; add halibut, herb side down. Cook for 5 minutes, or until browned. Flip fillets and place the pan in the oven for 10 minutes, or until fish is done.

Add onions to the squash and cook, covered, for 5 minutes, stirring occasionally. When squash is lightly browned, add wine and bay leaf. Cook until wine is absorbed. Add cream and nutmeg; cook until thickened. Season with salt and pepper. Toss in reserved herbs.

Spoon squash onto 4 plates and top with halibut and hazelnuts. Makes 4 servings.

PacificSeafood™

Cilantro Butter Tilapia Skillet Fillets
Regal Springs

1/4 teaspoon salt

1/4 teaspoon ground cumin

1/8 teaspoon ground red pepper

4 6-ounce Regal Springs tilapia fillets

Cooking spray

1 lemon, quartered

2 tablespoons butter, softened

2 tablespoons finely chopped fresh cilantro

1/2 teaspoon grated lemon peel

1/4 teaspoon paprika

1/8 teaspoon salt

Combine first 3 ingredients and sprinkle over both sides of fish.

Heat a large nonstick skillet over medium-high heat. Coat the pan and both sides of fish with cooking spray. Place fish in the pan and cook for 3 minutes on each side, or until it flakes easily with a fork.

Place the fish on a serving platter; squeeze lemon over the fish.

Place butter and remaining ingredients in a small bowl; stir until well blended. Serve with the fish. Makes 4 servings.

Chili Bean Sauce Tilapia
Tropical Aquaculture Products, Inc.

1 teaspoon chili bean paste
1/2 cup red wine vinegar
5 ounces unsalted butter, softened
2 tablespoons olive oil
4 5- to 7-ounce fresh Tropical Aquaculture* tilapia fillets
1/2 tablespoon flour
Salt and pepper

Combine chili bean paste and vinegar in a saucepan; bring to a boil and cook until reduced by half. Remove from the heat, add butter and stir until well blended.

Heat a frying pan over medium-high heat. Add olive oil.

Sprinkle both sides of tilapia fillets with flour and salt and pepper to taste. Sauté until golden brown, about 2 minutes per side.

Place tilapia on plates and spoon the sauce over the fillets. Makes 4 servings.

Brands may vary by region; substitute a similar product.

Ginger Orange Tilapia
Aquamericas

MARINADE
1 cup orange juice
1 teaspoon grated orange peel
1 teaspoon minced garlic
1 teaspoon grated fresh ginger
2 tablespoons vegetable oil

4 Mountain Stream* tilapia fillets
Flour seasoned with sea salt and pepper, for dredging
2 tablespoons vegetable oil
Thinly sliced green onions, for garnish

To prepare the marinade, in a small bowl, whisk together orange juice and peel, garlic, ginger and oil.

Place tilapia fillets in a shallow dish. Cover with the marinade and marinate for 20-30 minutes.

Remove tilapia from the marinade; reserve the marinade. Dredge tilapia in seasoned flour to coat, shaking off excess.

Heat 2 tablespoons oil in a large sauté pan over medium-high heat. Add tilapia and cook until lightly golden, 3-4 minutes on each side. Remove from the pan and keep warm.

Add remaining marinade to the pan, bring to a boil and cook for 1 minute. Reduce heat and simmer until it has a glaze consistency, 3-4 minutes.

Pour the sauce over the tilapia and garnish with green onions. Makes 4 servings.

Brands may vary by region; substitute a similar product.

aquamericas

Tilapia Fillets in Boursin Cream Sauce
Rain Forest Aquaculture

2 tablespoons butter

4 Rain Forest* fresh boneless, skinless tilapia fillets

1/2 cup flour seasoned with salt and pepper

1 tablespoon chopped fresh shallots

1/4 cup dry white wine

1/4 cup heavy cream

2 tablespoons Boursin cheese (sometimes available in Costco cheese section)

1 tablespoon chopped fresh parsley

Melt butter in a large sauté pan over medium heat.

Dredge fillets in the seasoned flour and sauté on the first side for 4 minutes, or until browned. Turn and cook for an additional 3 minutes, or until fillets flake easily with a fork. Place fillets on a plate and hold in a warm oven.

Add shallots and wine to the sauté pan and cook for 2 minutes, or until the volume of liquid is reduced by half. Add cream, bring the sauce to a boil and turn off the heat. Using a wire whisk, stir in Boursin until melted.

Place the warm fillets on plates, spoon some sauce over each and garnish with parsley. Makes 4 servings.

Brands may vary by region; substitute a similar product.

Rain Forest
AQUACULTURE
PRODUCTS, INC.

Toasted Crumb Tilapia with Roasted Red Pepper Aioli
Slade Gorton

1 ounce (2 tablespoons) unsalted butter

1 teaspoon lemon juice

4 fillets Slade Gorton* Toasted Crumb Tilapia

AIOLI

1/2 cup mayonnaise

1/4 cup roasted red pepper

1 teaspoon lemon juice

1 teaspoon Dijon mustard

1 teaspoon chopped shallot

Salt and pepper

Preheat oven to 325°F (375°F convection oven).

Melt butter either on the stove or in the microwave and mix with 1 teaspoon lemon juice. Lightly brush tilapia with the lemon butter.

Place tilapia on a parchment-lined baking sheet. Bake until the fish is flaky, approximately 8-10 minutes.

To prepare the aioli, combine mayonnaise, roasted red pepper, lemon juice, mustard, shallots, and salt and pepper to taste in a food processor (or use a handheld immersion blender). Blend until smooth.

Serve tilapia with the aioli. Makes 4 servings.

Brands may vary by region; substitute a similar product.

Tender Green Bean Stuffed Dover Sole with Green Chili Cream
Pacific Seafood Group

1 4-ounce can diced green chiles

1/4 cup white wine

1 garlic clove, minced

1/4 onion, chopped

Juice and grated peel of 1 lime

1 cup heavy whipping cream

1/2 pound fresh green beans, cleaned and blanched

8 Dover sole fillets

2 tablespoons toasted almonds

Fresh cilantro, for garnish

Preheat oven to 350°F.

In a large ovenproof sauté pan, heat green chiles, wine, garlic, onion, and lime juice and peel. Reduce over medium heat for 5 minutes, or until 3/4 of the wine is gone. Add cream and bring to a boil. Turn the heat down and continue cooking for 5 minutes.

Meanwhile, divide green beans into 8 bundles. Wrap a fillet of sole around each bundle of beans. Nestle the sole bundles in the sauté pan with the green chili cream. Spoon some of the cream over each sole fillet. Place the pan in the oven for about 10 minutes, or until the fish is cooked through.

Divide the sole among 4 plates. Return the pan to the stove, bring to a boil and reduce until the sauce is thickened.

Spoon the sauce over the fillets and garnish with toasted almonds and cilantro. Makes 4 servings.

Mediterranean Cod with Tossed Penne Pasta
Trident Seafoods

4 portions Trident Seafoods*
  Mediterranean Cod frozen fillets

4 ripe tomatoes, seeded and diced

3/4 cup kalamata olives

3/4 cup sun-dried tomatoes,
  chopped

3 tablespoons chopped fresh basil

2 tablespoons freshly chopped garlic

2 tablespoons balsamic vinegar

4 tablespoons extra-virgin olive oil

12 ounces penne pasta

Salt and ground pepper

3/4 cup fresh feta cheese crumbles

Preheat oven to 425°F.

Place frozen fish portions in a baking dish, tent loosely with foil and bake for 18-25 minutes, or until the fish flakes easily with the pressure of a fork.

In a large bowl, combine tomatoes, olives, sun-dried tomatoes, basil, garlic, vinegar and olive oil.

Cook penne in boiling salted water until al dente, about 10-12 minutes. Drain. Add to the tomato mixture and toss. Season to taste with salt and pepper.

Spoon blended pasta into large individual serving bowls, add the cod and top with feta. Makes 4 servings.

* Brands may vary by region; substitute a similar product.

Cedar-Planked
Bourbon-Glazed Catfish
American Pride Seafoods

4 cedar planks
4 American Pride*
    fresh catfish fillets
    (24 ounces)
1 teaspoon chopped
    fresh parsley

BOURBON GLAZE
1/4 cup bourbon
1/2 cup orange
    marmalade
1 cup barbecue sauce

Soak the cedar planks overnight in water. Place them on a preheated grill for about 10 minutes, or until they begin to char and smoke. Turn to the other side and repeat.

To prepare the glaze, combine bourbon, marmalade and barbecue sauce in a saucepan. Warm over medium heat to incorporate the marmalade.

Lightly brush catfish fillets with the glaze and place on the smoldering planks. Cover with foil. Cook on the grill for 4-6 minutes, or until the fish is white and flaky.

Coat the fish again with the bourbon glaze, sprinkle with parsley and serve hot on the planks. Serve with your favorite rice side dish. Makes 4 servings.

* Brands may vary by region; substitute a similar product.

Thai Catfish
Delta Pride Catfish

4 tablespoons soy sauce
3 tablespoons toasted
    sesame oil, divided
1 tablespoon rice
    wine vinegar
3 limes, juiced, strips
    of peel reserved
    for garnish
1/4 teaspoon red
    pepper flakes
2 tablespoons minced
    fresh ginger
2 garlic cloves, minced
1/2 cup chopped
    fresh cilantro
6 3- to 5-ounce Delta
    Pride* catfish fillets
2 cups thinly sliced
    shiitake mushrooms
1/4 cup peanut oil (or
    sesame or canola oil)
Cilantro, for garnish
Cooked rice or Asian-style
    noodles (optional)

In a bowl, combine soy sauce, 2 tablespoons sesame oil, vinegar, lime juice, red pepper flakes, ginger, garlic and chopped cilantro. Set aside 3 tablespoons of the marinade for the mushrooms. Add catfish to the remaining marinade and set aside to marinate for 15-30 minutes.

Soak mushrooms in the reserved marinade mixture.

Heat 1 tablespoon sesame oil in a sauté pan over medium heat. Add mushrooms and sauté for 5 minutes. Set aside.

In a separate sauté pan, heat peanut oil over medium heat. Add catfish and marinade to the pan. Sauté catfish for 5-6 minutes on each side, or until it flakes. Add mushrooms to the catfish and garnish with lime peel and cilantro.

Serve over rice or Asian-style noodles.
Makes 6 servings.

* Brands may vary by region; substitute a similar product.

Pistachio-Crusted New England Flounder
North Coast Seafoods

½ cup roasted pistachio nuts
½ cup plain dry bread crumbs
1 teaspoon chopped garlic
1 tablespoon chopped fresh parsley
1 teaspoon freshly cracked pepper
1 teaspoon kosher salt

2 eggs
Olive oil
4 2- to 4-ounce fresh North Coast Seafoods* flounder fillets
½ cup all-purpose flour
1 lemon, cut into wedges

Combine the first 6 ingredients in a food processor and pulse until incorporated and the nuts are chopped. Transfer to a shallow bowl.

Place eggs in a shallow bowl and beat.

Heat olive oil in a cast iron skillet over medium heat.

Dredge each fillet in flour, then in the egg and then in the bread crumb mixture. Make sure the fish has a nice coating of bread crumbs.

Place fillets in the pan and cook until crispy, about 3 minutes per side.

Serve with lemon wedges. Makes 2 servings.

Brands may vary by region; substitute a similar product.

Trout with Mediterranean Vegetable Medley
Clear Springs

4 Clear Springs* dressed trout

Salt and pepper

Flour for dusting

2 tablespoons olive oil

VEGETABLE MEDLEY

2 tablespoons olive oil

2 cups sliced fresh mushrooms

1 cup halved and thinly sliced red onion

2 garlic cloves, finely chopped

4 teaspoons white wine

2 tablespoons lemon juice

1/2 cup mini plum tomatoes, halved

1 14-ounce can quartered artichoke hearts, rinsed and drained

Salt and pepper

2 tablespoons minced fresh parsley, for garnish

Season trout with salt and pepper to taste. Dredge in flour.

Heat 2 tablespoons olive oil in a sauté pan over medium heat. Add trout and cook for 7 minutes per side, or until it reaches an internal temperature of 140°F.

To prepare the vegetable medley, heat olive oil in another sauté pan over medium heat. Add mushrooms and cook until browned, then stir in onions and garlic; continue sautéing until onions are translucent, about 3 minutes.

Stir in wine and lemon juice. Add tomatoes, artichoke hearts, and salt and pepper to taste; cook until liquid is reduced by half.

Place trout and vegetable medley on plates. Garnish with parsley. Makes 4 servings.

Brands may vary by region; substitute a similar product.

Zesty Marinated Baked Rainbow Trout
Idaho Trout

4 Idaho Trout* whole dressed rainbow trout

Zesty Italian salad dressing

Salt and pepper

Lemon pepper

Garlic salt (optional)

1 medium yellow or white onion, chopped (optional)

2 tablespoons butter or margarine, melted

Marinate trout in Italian dressing in the refrigerator overnight.

Preheat oven to 350°F.

Place trout in a well-greased shallow baking dish; discard marinade. Season trout cavities with salt, pepper and garlic salt to taste. Fill the cavities partially with onions.

Drizzle melted butter over the fish.

Cover the dish with aluminum foil and bake, removing the foil after 20 minutes. Bake until the fish flakes easily with a fork, 5-6 minutes for each 1/2 inch of thickness. Makes 4 servings.

Brands may vary by region; substitute a similar product.

Tuscan Seafood Stew
Kirkland Signature/Filippo Berio

3/4 cup Kirkland Signature/Filippo Berio Organic Extra Virgin Olive Oil ♥Organic

1 large red onion, coarsely chopped

4 large garlic cloves, minced

1 1/2 teaspoons red pepper flakes

1 cup dry red wine

1 28-ounce can crushed plum tomatoes

1/2 cup minced fresh flat-leaf parsley, divided

1 1/2 teaspoons salt

24 littleneck clams

24 medium or large peeled shrimp

2-2 1/2 pounds mild white-fleshed fish fillets, cut into 2-inch chunks

3 cups cold water

6-8 thick slices crusty Italian bread, toasted

Heat olive oil in a 6-quart Dutch oven over medium heat. Add onion, garlic and red pepper. Cook, stirring occasionally, for 10 minutes, or until soft.

Add wine. Increase the heat to medium-high and cook at a brisk simmer for 5 minutes, or until the wine no longer smells of alcohol.

Add tomatoes, all but 2 tablespoons of parsley and salt. Bring to a boil, then reduce the heat until the sauce simmers gently. Cover and cook for 10 minutes, stirring occasionally.

Add clams and shrimp; stir. Add fish and stir gently. Increase the heat to high. Cook for 2 minutes, or until the liquid starts to bubble. Add water. Cover and reduce the heat so the mixture simmers but does not boil. Cook for 10 minutes, or until the clams open and the other seafood is opaque in the center. Discard any clams that do not open.

Set the bread in pasta plates or large shallow bowls and spoon the stew over it. Sprinkle with the remaining parsley. Makes 6-8 servings.

Day Boat Haddock "Gloucester Style"
North Coast Seafoods

3 pounds North Coast Seafoods* skinless haddock fillets

Kosher salt and pepper

2 tablespoons olive oil

1 medium onion, thinly sliced

1 tablespoon chopped fresh garlic

2 teaspoons freshly squeezed lemon juice

6 slices white bread, cut into 1/2-inch cubes

2 tablespoons chopped fresh parsley

1 tablespoon chopped fresh oregano

Preheat oven to 350°F.

Place haddock in a single layer in a greased baking dish. Season to taste with salt and pepper.

Heat olive oil in a skillet over medium heat. Add onions and garlic and sauté until soft.

In a bowl, combine the remaining ingredients. Stir in onions and garlic.

Spread the bread mixture over the haddock and bake for 20 minutes, or until the fish flakes and the bread cubes are toasted. Makes 6 servings.

Brands may vary by region; substitute a similar product.

Cara Cara/Clementine Salsa
Cecelia Packing/AMC Direct

2 large Cecelia Packing* Cara Cara oranges

2 medium AMC Direct* clementines

2 tablespoons finely diced shallots

1 teaspoon kosher salt

Freshly ground black pepper

1/3 cup extra-virgin olive oil

1 teaspoon minced fresh savory

1 tablespoon sliced fresh mint

2 tablespoons chopped fresh flat-leaf parsley

Lemon juice

Cut both ends off the Cara Caras and clementines. Place the fruit cut side down on a cutting board. Following the contour of the fruit with your knife, remove the peel and white cottony pith, working from top to bottom and rotating the fruit as you go. Then hold each piece of fruit over a bowl and carefully slice between the membranes and the fruit to release the segments. You should have about a cup of segments and a cup of juice.

Place the fruit juice in a small bowl and add shallots, salt and pepper to taste. Let sit for 5 minutes. Slowly whisk in olive oil.

Stir in the fruit segments, savory, mint and parsley. Add a little lemon juice for flavor. Taste for balance and seasoning.

Serve with grilled fish. Makes 6-8 servings.

Brands may vary by region; substitute a similar product.

Creamy Pistachio Pesto over Whole Wheat Pasta
Kirkland Signature/Setton Pistachio/ Setton Farms

15 ounces whole-wheat penne pasta

1/3 cup plus 2 tablespoons extra-virgin olive oil, divided

8 cloves roasted garlic, or 6 cloves raw garlic

3 tablespoons lemon juice

1/2 cup Kirkland Signature* roasted, salted California pistachio nuts, shelled, plus 2 tablespoons for garnish

2 1/2 cups packed fresh basil leaves, plus sprig for garnish

1 tablespoon light miso paste, or 3 tablespoons grated Parmesan cheese

1/2 teaspoon sea salt

1/2 teaspoon freshly ground pepper

1 cup cherry tomatoes, sliced in half lengthwise

1/2 cup pitted kalamata olives, sliced into thirds

Cook pasta according to package directions. Drain, transfer to a bowl and toss to coat with 2 tablespoons olive oil; set aside.

To prepare the pesto, place garlic, 1/3 cup olive oil and lemon juice in a food processor and blend for 15 seconds. Add 1/2 cup pistachios, basil, miso, salt and pepper; blend for 30 seconds, or until smooth.

Add pesto to the pasta and toss to coat. Add tomatoes and olives. Adjust seasoning. Garnish with a basil sprig and remaining pistachios. Serve warm. Makes 6 servings.

Tip: To roast garlic, preheat oven to 375°F. Wrap a garlic bulb in foil, with a dash of olive oil. Roast for 30 minutes, or until the cloves are soft.

Recipe courtesy of Chef Jenny Goldberg, www.sporkfoods.com, 2008.
* Brands may vary by region; substitute a similar product.

Baked Ziti
New York Style Sausage

2 tablespoons olive oil

1 tablespoon crushed garlic

1 tablespoon finely chopped shallot

³/₄ pound New York Style* bulk sausage

¹/₂ teaspoon salt

¹/₂ teaspoon ground black pepper

1 ¹/₂ cups diced eggplant

1 ¹/₂ cups diced brown mushrooms

¹/₄ cup white wine

¹/₄ cup chicken stock

2 tablespoons chopped fresh basil

¹/₂ of 8-ounce container part-skim ricotta cheese

³/₄ cup shredded mild provolone cheese

1 ¹/₂ cups crushed tomatoes in puree (or your favorite pasta sauce)

8 ounces ziti or penne pasta, cooked according to package directions

¹/₄ cup grated Romano or Parmesan cheese

¹/₂ cup shredded smoked provolone cheese

Preheat oven to 350°F.

In a preheated nonstick skillet over medium heat, sauté olive oil, garlic, shallots and sausage for 2-3 minutes, or until lightly browned.

Add salt, pepper, eggplant and mushrooms; sauté for another 1-2 minutes.

Turn heat up to high, add wine and stir until evaporated. Add chicken stock and cook until slightly reduced. Return heat to medium and simmer for 1-2 more minutes.

Gently fold in basil, ricotta, mild provolone and tomatoes. Simmer for 1-2 minutes.

Fold in cooked pasta and Romano or Parmesan cheese.

Transfer to a casserole and top with smoked provolone. Bake for 8-10 minutes, or until heated through. Makes 4 servings.

Brands may vary by region; substitute a similar product.

Mushroom Ragu
Giorgio Foods

1 tablespoon olive oil

1 tablespoon butter

¹/₂ cup chopped onion

¹/₂ tablespoon minced garlic

4 4-ounce cans Giorgio, Brandywine or Penn Dutch* mushrooms, drained

1 teaspoon dried thyme

1 teaspoon dried marjoram

2 teaspoons flour

¹/₂ cup dry white wine

1 14 ¹/₂-ounce can diced tomatoes

2 tablespoons tomato paste

1 ¹/₂ cups vegetable or chicken stock

2 tablespoons plain yogurt

³/₄ teaspoon salt

¹/₈ teaspoon ground black pepper

Pasta or polenta

Heat olive oil and butter in a large Dutch oven over medium heat. When the butter starts to foam, add onion and cook until translucent but not browned. Add garlic and cook for about 30 seconds.

Add mushrooms, thyme and marjoram, and cook, stirring frequently, for about 10 minutes.

Stir in flour. Add wine and cook for about 10 minutes to reduce.

Add tomatoes, tomato paste, stock, yogurt, salt and pepper. Continue to simmer, stirring occasionally, until the liquid is reduced and the mixture thickened.

This ragu can be served over pasta and is particularly good over store-bought polenta that has been sliced and sautéed in olive oil. It's also excellent over homemade polenta. Serve hot. Makes 4-6 servings.

Brands may vary by region; substitute a similar product.

Penne with Sausage and Roasted Peppers
Premio

5 red bell peppers

4 tablespoons olive oil, divided

2 onions, cut in 1-inch dice

3 tablespoons minced garlic

8 links Premio* sweet Italian sausage, casings removed

2 tablespoons chopped fresh rosemary

1 14-ounce can plum tomatoes, roughly crushed

Salt and pepper

1 pound penne, cooked al dente and drained

Grated Parmesan cheese

Preheat oven to 425°F.

Roast peppers until skin blackens and blisters. Transfer to a bowl and cover with plastic wrap. Let cool for 30 minutes. Remove skin, stem and seeds. Cut in 1-inch squares and reserve.

Heat 2 tablespoons olive oil in a large heavy-bottomed saucepan. Add onions and sauté over medium heat until tender. Add peppers and cook until soft. Add garlic and cook for 5 minutes. Remove from the pan.

Add remaining 2 tablespoons olive oil to the pan and brown sausage meat, breaking up with a spoon, for 10 minutes, or until cooked. Add pepper mixture and rosemary. Stir in tomatoes, bring to a simmer and cook for 7-8 minutes. Season with salt and pepper to taste.

Combine cooked pasta with sausage mixture and heat through.

Serve with grated Parmesan. Makes 6 servings.

Brands may vary by region; substitute a similar product.

Italian Sausage Calzone
Classico

1 pound bulk Italian sausage

1 cup assorted toppings, such as sliced jalapeños, olives or mushrooms, fresh spinach, roasted yellow peppers, hot pepper rings and sautéed onions

Nonstick cooking spray

1 13.8-ounce can refrigerated pizza crust dough

1 cup shredded four-cheese Italian blend

1 32-ounce jar Classico* Tomato & Basil Pasta Sauce, divided

1 tablespoon milk

2 tablespoons grated Parmesan cheese

Preheat oven to 400°F.

In a large skillet, cook sausage over medium heat for 8-10 minutes, or until browned and cooked through. Stir in toppings and remove from the heat.

Coat a baking sheet with cooking spray. Unroll pizza dough onto the baking sheet and carefully stretch to form a circle. Layer the sausage mixture and shredded cheese on one-half of the crust, leaving a 1-inch border. Add half of the pasta sauce, reserving half for dipping. Gently fold the crust over the filling. Seal the edges by crimping with fingertips or pressing with a fork. Cut 2 to 3 slits on top. Brush with milk and sprinkle with Parmesan.

Bake for 20-25 minutes, or until the crust is golden brown. Let stand for 5 minutes. Serve with the reserved pasta sauce. Makes 4-6 servings.

Tips: This can be prepared in advance, covered and refrigerated. When you're ready to serve, brush with milk, sprinkle with Parmesan and bake. To spice it up, sprinkle sausage with red pepper flakes. For the meat-lover's version, substitute sliced pepperoni and ham for the toppings.

* Brands may vary by region; substitute a similar product.

Tuna and Basil Penne
Kirkland Signature

1 can Kirkland Signature albacore, drained

3 tablespoons extra-virgin olive oil

1 garlic clove, minced

1 teaspoon lemon juice

1 tablespoon finely grated lemon peel

1/4 cup packed fresh basil leaves, julienned

8 ounces penne pasta, uncooked

Salt and pepper

In a large bowl, toss together albacore, olive oil, garlic, lemon juice and peel, and basil.

Cook penne according to package directions and drain in a colander.

Add penne to the albacore mixture and toss with salt and pepper to taste. Makes 2 servings.

Four-Cheese Ravioli with Roasted Eggplant Sauce
Kirkland Signature/Seviroli Foods

2 medium eggplants, cut into 1/2-inch cubes

8 ripe tomatoes, sliced thin

3 garlic cloves, sliced thin

1/2 cup olive oil

2 teaspoons salt

1 teaspoon ground black pepper

1/4 cup chopped basil

1 24-ounce jar of your favorite marinara sauce

36 Kirkland Signature frozen Four-Cheese Ravioli

1/2 cup ricotta cheese

Grated Romano cheese

Preheat oven to 400°F.

In a large bowl, combine eggplant, tomatoes, garlic, olive oil, salt and pepper. Stir to mix well. Spread evenly on a baking sheet and roast in the oven for 30-45 minutes, stirring occasionally, or until the eggplant and tomatoes are tender and nicely browned. Transfer to a food processor; add basil and pulse chop for 30 seconds.

Place marinara sauce in a pot and bring to a simmer. Add the eggplant mixture and cook, stirring, for 5 minutes.

Cook ravioli according to package directions.

Divide ravioli among 6 bowls. Top with the eggplant sauce and garnish with a tablespoon of ricotta and a sprinkle of Romano. Makes 6 servings.

Spinach Ravioli with Smoked Salmon in Pesto Cream Sauce
Cibo Naturals/Monterey Gourmet Foods

6 ounces smoked wild salmon (lox style)

19 ounces Monterey Pasta Company "Made with Organic" Spinach and Cheese Ravioli

1 cup heavy cream

1 1/2 cups Kirkland Signature/ Cibo Naturals Basil Pesto

2 tablespoons grated Parmigiano-Reggiano cheese

2 tablespoons finely chopped fresh basil (optional)

Fill a large stockpot with 4 quarts of water and bring to a boil over high heat.

While the water heats, cut smoked salmon into bite-size strips, reserving 2 tablespoons for garnish.

When the water comes to a boil, add ravioli and cook according to package directions for 5 minutes.

While the ravioli is cooking, add cream to a medium saucepan and place over medium heat. When the cream begins to bubble, reduce heat to low and cook to reduce.

Just before draining the ravioli, turn the heat off under the cream and stir in pesto and smoked salmon (reserving 2 tablespoons).

When the ravioli is ready, drain thoroughly.

To serve, spoon half of the sauce onto a warm serving platter. Arrange ravioli on top and spoon the remaining sauce over the top. Garnish with Parmigiano-Reggiano, remaining strips of smoked salmon and basil. Makes 5 servings.

Spicy Sausage Penne with Red Pepper Sauce
Windset Farms

RED PEPPER SAUCE
1/4 cup butter

3 shallots, minced

3 Windset Farms Misto* red bell peppers, seeded and chopped

1 1/2 teaspoons kosher salt

1 tablespoon sugar

1 1/2 tablespoons rice vinegar

1 cup chicken or vegetable stock

3 tablespoons extra-virgin olive oil

4 spicy Italian sausages, casings removed

1 large garlic clove, finely minced

1 pound penne

2 tablespoons finely chopped basil

1/4 cup finely grated Parmesan cheese

To prepare the red pepper sauce, place a skillet over medium/low heat and add butter. When butter melts, add shallots, peppers and salt. Sauté until just soft, about 7 minutes. Add sugar and vinegar and reduce until syrupy, about 4 minutes. Add stock and bring to a boil. Simmer for 5 minutes. Remove the sauce from the heat and puree in a blender.

Place a skillet over medium heat and add olive oil. Add sausage and garlic; cook until sausage is browned, stirring to crumble into pieces. Drain off excess oil. Add the pureed red pepper sauce and simmer for 2 minutes.

Fill a large stockpot with salted water; bring to a boil. Add pasta and boil until al dente, about 10 minutes. Drain in a colander.

Toss pasta with the red pepper and sausage sauce and chopped basil. Top with grated Parmesan and serve. Makes 4 servings.

Tip: This red pepper sauce also makes a great accompaniment for grilled chicken or seared halibut.

* Brands may vary by region; substitute a similar product.

Meatballs
Kirkland Signature/Orleans International

1 cup plain bread crumbs
1/2 pound hot pork sausage
2 1/2 pounds Kirkland Signature ground beef
2 eggs

1 cup milk
1 teaspoon garlic salt
1/4 teaspoon pepper
1/4 cup grated Parmesan cheese

Preheat broiler to high.

Mix all ingredients together in a large bowl.

Form into 1- to 2-inch balls and line up on a broiler pan. Broil until browned on top. Turn the meatballs over and brown on the other side.

Simmer in your favorite spaghetti sauce and serve with pasta, or serve plain with sauce options on the side as an appetizer. Makes 6 servings.

Fettuccine with Roasted Chicken and Lemon Cream Sauce
Pacific Natural Foods

1 pound boneless, skinless chicken thigh meat

2 tablespoons olive oil, plus more for coating chicken

Salt and pepper

1 pound fettuccine noodles

2 tablespoons minced garlic

1 small shallot, minced

1/2 cup dry white wine

2 cups Pacific Natural Foods* Organic Free Range Chicken Broth ♥Organic

2 cups heavy cream

1/2 bunch Italian parsley, chopped

Juice and grated peel of 1 lemon

1/2 cup grated Parmigiano-Reggiano cheese

Preheat oven to 350°F.

Place chicken in a roasting pan and thinly coat with olive oil. Season to taste with salt and pepper. Roast chicken for 45 minutes, or until cooked. Let cool and shred/slice into thin strips.

Prepare pasta according to package directions.

In a large sauté pan, heat 2 tablespoons olive oil over medium-high heat. Add garlic and shallots and sauté, taking care not to brown. Add wine and cook until reduced by half. Add chicken broth and cream; simmer over medium-high heat, stirring occasionally, until the sauce begins to thicken.

Add chicken, parsley, lemon juice and grated peel, and salt and pepper to taste.

Combine with pasta. Serve with grated Parmigiano-Reggiano. Makes 4 servings.

Brands may vary by region; substitute a similar product.

King Crab Fettuccine
Harbor Seafood

1 pound Oyster Bay Brand* frozen king crab legs and claws, thawed and drained (6-8 ounces crabmeat)

1/2 cup butter or margarine

1 garlic clove, minced

3/4 cup heavy cream

1/2 cup grated Parmesan cheese

1/2 teaspoon freshly ground black pepper

12 ounces fettuccine pasta, cooked and drained

1 tablespoon chopped fresh parsley

Salt

Slice crab legs and claws lengthwise and cut into small pieces. Remove the meat from the shells.

Melt butter in a saucepan over medium heat. Add garlic and sauté until lightly browned. Blend in crabmeat, heavy cream, Parmesan and black pepper. Cook, stirring gently, until thoroughly heated.

Add the crab mixture to the cooked fettuccine and toss lightly. Garnish with parsley. Add salt to taste. Makes 6 servings.

Brands may vary by region; substitute a similar product.

Easy Pasta Primavera
Del Monte Foods

6 ounces dry spaghetti

1 cup small broccoli florets

1 14 1/2-ounce can Del Monte, Contadina or S&W* Italian stewed tomatoes

1 14 1/2-ounce can Del Monte or S&W* cut green beans, drained

2 cups cubed cooked chicken or turkey

Shaved Parmesan cheese (optional)

Cook pasta according to package directions, adding broccoli for the last 3 minutes of cooking; drain.

Meanwhile, combine undrained tomatoes and beans in a large skillet. Bring to a boil, then reduce heat. Cook, uncovered, for 2 minutes. Stir in chicken and heat through.

Transfer the pasta and broccoli to a serving platter. Top with the tomato mixture. Toss before serving. Garnish with shaved Parmesan cheese, if desired. Makes 4 servings.

* Brands may vary by region; substitute a similar product.

Veggie Quiche
Eat Smart

1 prepared 9-inch piecrust

2 tablespoons Dijon-
style mustard

2 1/2 cups Eat Smart*
broccoli florets

1 cup shredded Swiss cheese

1/3 cup chopped
green onions

3 eggs

1 cup milk

Salt and pepper (optional)

Preheat oven according to piecrust package directions.

Spread mustard on the bottom and sides of the piecrust. Bake for 10 minutes. Remove from the oven.

Place broccoli, cheese and green onions in the piecrust, mixing well.

In a small bowl, combine eggs, milk, and salt and pepper to taste. Pour over the vegetable mixture.

Bake in a 400°F oven for 35-40 minutes, or until the center is set and the top is browned. Let stand for 20 minutes before cutting. Makes 4-6 servings.

Brands may vary by region; substitute a similar product.

Famous Mushroom Quiche
Cardile Brothers

1 unbaked 9-inch pie shell

4 cups sliced fresh Cardile
Brothers* mushrooms

1 tablespoon butter

1 cup shredded
Swiss cheese

2 tablespoons flour

3 eggs, lightly beaten

1 1/4 cups milk

1 tablespoon minced
fresh parsley

1 teaspoon garlic salt

1/2 teaspoon pepper

Preheat oven to 425°F.

Bake pie shell for 10 minutes; remove and let cool.

Reduce oven heat to 350°F.

Sauté mushrooms in butter over medium-high heat until tender. Remove from the pan with a slotted spoon and set aside.

In a bowl, toss cheese with flour; add eggs, milk, parsley, garlic salt and pepper. Stir in mushrooms. Pour into the crust.

Bake for 1 hour, or until set, covering edges with foil to prevent overbrowning, if needed. Let stand for 10 minutes before cutting. Makes 6 servings.

Brands may vary by region; substitute a similar product.

Fontina and Fuji Apple Croissant with Baby Greens
Vie de France

1 large Vie de France butter croissant

2 thick slices Fontina cheese

1/4 cup baby greens

1/2 Fuji apple, cored and sliced

2 tablespoons candied walnuts or pecans

Preheat oven to 325°F.

Slice croissant in half. Place a cheese slice on each half. Bake until the cheese is melted, approximately 10 minutes.

Remove from the oven and place a layer of baby greens and sliced apples on each croissant half.

Top with candied nuts and serve open-face. Makes 1 serving.

Tip: To prevent apple slices from turning brown, place in water with lemon juice if not using immediately.

Avocado Ranch Salad Wraps
Willow Brook

1 avocado, cut in 1/2-inch dice

2 teaspoons fresh lime juice

1/2 cup ranch dressing

Salt and pepper

1 pound Willow Brook* Kettle Fried Turkey Breast

4 cups mixed salad greens

4 10-inch flour tortillas (use your favorite flavor)

12 grape tomatoes, halved

1/4 cup chopped cilantro

1/4 cup sliced red onion

3 tablespoons shredded extra-sharp white Cheddar cheese

Combine avocado, lime juice and ranch dressing. Season to taste with salt and pepper.

Shred turkey and stir into the avocado mixture.

Place salad greens on tortillas, followed by the dressed shredded turkey, tomatoes, cilantro, onion and cheese. Roll up the wraps and cut in half. Makes 4 servings.

Brands may vary by region; substitute a similar product.

Grilled Veggie Wraps
Sabra Go Mediterranean

1 medium zucchini, cut in
    half lengthwise

1 medium yellow squash, cut in
    half lengthwise

1 medium red bell pepper

1 medium green bell pepper

Olive oil

Salt and black pepper

2 8-inch herbed or spinach wraps

Sabra* Roasted Garlic Hummus

1/2 cup shredded fresh spinach
    leaves

Drizzle zucchini, squash and peppers with olive oil and season to taste with salt and pepper. Grill, turning frequently, until outer skins of peppers are charred and zucchini and squash are almost cooked through. Remove from the grill and let cool.

Spread each wrap with 2 heaping tablespoons hummus. Sprinkle evenly with spinach.

Peel roasted peppers and remove stems and seeds. Slice into thin strips. Slice zucchini and squash thinly on the diagonal. Arrange grilled vegetables over hummus and spinach in center of wraps.

To form the wraps, roll one end in and tuck both sides while rolling. Squeeze as you roll to keep the shape. Secure with toothpicks and slice in half on the diagonal. Makes 2 servings.

Brands may vary by region; substitute a similar product.

Cold Vegetarian Sandwich
Cottage Bakery

1 Kirkland Signature*
   ciabatta roll

1 ½ tablespoons roasted
   garlic mayonnaise

4-6 spinach leaves

3-4 tomato slices

Red onion, thinly sliced

2 pieces thinly sliced
   provolone cheese
   (optional)

2 lengthwise slices
   cucumber

½ avocado, sliced

½ ounce alfalfa sprouts

Slice ciabatta roll in half. Spread mayonnaise on both halves.

On the bottom half of the ciabatta, in the order listed, place spinach, tomato, red onion, provolone, cucumber, avocado and alfalfa sprouts. Add top half of ciabatta. Makes 1 serving.

Tip: To make roasted garlic mayonnaise, mix ¼ cup roasted garlic with 1 cup mayonnaise.

Brands may vary by region; substitute a similar product.

Antipasto Sandwich
Cottage Bakery

1 Kirkland Signature*
   demi baguette loaf

½ tablespoon mustard

8-9 arugula leaves

1 ounce prosciutto

1 ounce salami

1 ounce capicola

Sliced provolone (optional)

2-3 tomato slices

6-8 black olive slices

4-6 marinated artichoke
   hearts, quartered

1 pepperoncini, sliced

½ tablespoon olive oil

½ tablespoon vinegar

Salt and pepper

1 tablespoon mayonnaise

Slice bread in half lengthwise. Spread mustard on the bottom half.

In the order listed, top with arugula, prosciutto, salami, capicola, provolone, tomato, black olives, artichoke hearts and pepperoncini.

Drizzle with oil and vinegar. Season to taste with salt and pepper.

Spread mayonnaise on top half of bread and close the sandwich. Makes 1 serving.

Brands may vary by region; substitute a similar product.

Smoked Ham, Spicy Mayo and Avocado Sandwich
La Brea Bakery

2 slices La Brea Bakery*
   Whole Grain Loaf
4 ounces sliced smoked ham
1/2 medium-size avocado
1 tablespoon arugula

SPICY MAYO
2 garlic cloves
1 7-ounce can chipotle peppers in
   adobo sauce
1/4 cup chopped fresh cilantro
Juice of 1 lime
4 cups mayonnaise

To prepare the spicy mayo, combine garlic, chipotles, cilantro and lime juice in a food processor and blend until smooth. Mix with mayonnaise.

Spread 2 tablespoons of spicy mayo on one side of bread slices. Fold the ham slices and layer unevenly across one of the bread slices. Fan out the avocado by slicing it, and spread across the ham. Top with arugula and the second slice of bread.
Makes 1 serving.

Brands may vary by region; substitute a similar product.

Smoked Gouda Tuna Melt
Chicken of the Sea

2 6-ounce cans Chicken of the Sea* Solid White Tuna in Water

1 8-ounce package cream cheese, softened

8 ounces smoked Gouda cheese, grated

8 slices favorite bread

4 slices tomato

8 slices crisply cooked bacon

Butter, softened

Open tuna, drain and flake; set aside.

In a food processor, blend cream cheese and Gouda.

Stir tuna and cheese mixture together until blended.

Divide the tuna mixture and spread evenly on 4 slices of bread. Top each with 1 tomato slice, 2 bacon slices and second slice of bread.

Lightly butter outside of bread and grill until golden brown on both sides.

Serve with soup or fresh fruit. Makes 4 servings.

Brands may vary by region; substitute a similar product.

Gourmet Panini Sandwiches
Daniele

4 ciabatta rolls

Olive oil

1 16-ounce package Daniele* Gourmet Presliced Variety Pack (Hot Calabrese, Hot Capocollo, Peppered Genoa Salame)

1 large ball fresh mozzarella

4 ounces roasted peppers

4 basil leaves

Slice ciabatta rolls in half horizontally. Drizzle with olive oil.

Place 4 ounces of assorted sliced meats on each roll.

Slice mozzarella and place 1 or 2 slices on each roll.

Top with roasted peppers and basil.

Eat as is or grill in a panini maker. Makes 4 servings.

Brands may vary by region; substitute a similar product.

Desserts

Apricot Martini
Trinity Fruit

APRICOTS
2 tablespoons butter

4 cups halved and pitted Trinity Fruit apricots

2 cups sugar

3 tablespoons cornstarch

CRUST
1 1/4 cups all-purpose flour

1/2 teaspoon salt

1 tablespoon sugar

1/3 cup vegetable shortening

2 egg whites, divided

3-4 tablespoons ice-cold water

1/2 teaspoon white vinegar

1/2 pint heavy whipping cream

1/4 cup confectioners' sugar

Fresh mint sprigs

Light corn syrup

4 tablespoons sugar

4 martini glasses

To prepare the apricots, melt butter in a medium saucepan over medium heat. Add apricots. Mix sugar and cornstarch together and stir into the apricots. Cook, stirring, until thickened and apricots are soft.

Preheat oven to 450°F.

To prepare the crust, combine flour, salt and sugar in a bowl. Use a pastry blender to cut shortening into dry ingredients until the mixture resembles small peas. In a separate bowl, combine 1 egg white, water and vinegar. Pour into the dry mixture and stir to form a ball. Roll out the dough on a floured board. Cut into 8 shapes with a cookie-cutter.

Place cut-out shapes on an ungreased cookie sheet and brush with egg white.

Bake for 5 minutes, or until golden brown.

Beat cream and confectioners' sugar in a bowl until it forms peaks.

Brush mint leaves with corn syrup, then sprinkle with sugar.

To serve, place 5 or 6 warm apricots in each martini glass. Add 2 baked shapes. Top with whipped cream and a mint sprig. Makes 4 servings.

Created by Lisa and Patricia White.

Black and Blue Party Trifle
Sun Belle

2 boxes vanilla instant pudding mix (3.4 ounces each)

4 cups milk

1/4 cup orange juice

2 teaspoons lemon juice

1 teaspoon vanilla extract

1 16-ounce pound cake

18 ounces Sun Belle* blackberries (4 cups), plus more for garnish

24 ounces Sun Belle* blueberries (5 cups), plus more for garnish

1 14- to 15-ounce aerosol can whipped cream

Fresh mint, for garnish

Prepare pudding according to package directions, using milk.

Mix orange and lemon juices with vanilla.

Cut cake into 1/2-inch cubes (about 120 pieces).

Layer a third of the cake pieces in the bottom of a 4-quart glass bowl. Spoon a third of the juice mix over cake. Scatter a third of berries over the moistened cake, placing berries along outer edge of bowl to highlight layering. Spread a third of pudding over berries. Spray a 1-inch layer of whipped cream over berries. Repeat with 2 more layers.

Decorate the final whipped cream layer with berries and mint sprigs. Makes 16-24 servings.

Tips: If the bowl flares out, use less cake and pudding in the first layer and more in the third. Alternatively, spoon prepared trifle into stemmed glasses for an elegant presentation.

* Brands may vary by region; substitute a similar product.

Fruitables Orange Passion Pudding Delight
Apple & Eve

1/4 cup sugar

1 envelope unflavored gelatin

1 1/2 cups Apple & Eve* Fruitables Orange Passion 100% Juice

1 cup mandarin oranges, thoroughly drained, plus more for garnish

1/2 cup heavy cream

4 ounces whipped topping

Mix sugar and gelatin in a small bowl.

Place 1/2 cup juice in a small saucepan. Sprinkle with the gelatin mixture; let stand for 1 minute. Stir over low heat until the gelatin dissolves (do not bring to a boil). Remove from the heat and set aside to cool. Stir in remaining 1 cup juice.

In a blender, puree 1 cup mandarin oranges. Gently stir in gelatin mixture, then slowly add heavy cream until combined.

Pour the mixture into decorative glasses or ramekins. Refrigerate, stirring occasionally after 1 hour, then let set overnight.

Garnish with whipped topping and mandarin orange slices. Makes 4 servings.

Brands may vary by region; substitute a similar product.

Cherry Muscat Compote with Panna Cotta
M&R Company

PANNA COTTA

2 teaspoons unflavored gelatin

1 1/2 cups heavy cream

6 tablespoons sugar

1/2 cup whole milk

6 3 1/2-ounce ramekins, chilled

CHERRY MUSCAT COMPOTE

1/2 cup plus 1 teaspoon sugar, divided

1 tablespoon light corn syrup

1 vanilla bean, halved lengthwise

3 cups pitted fresh M&R cherries

1 tablespoon lemon juice

1/2 cup Woodbridge Muscat dessert wine

To prepare panna cotta, place 3 tablespoons cold water in a stainless-steel bowl. Sprinkle with gelatin; let stand for 5 minutes.

Combine cream and sugar in a saucepan and stir over medium-high heat until sugar dissolves and bubbles form at edges, about 2 minutes.

Place bowl with gelatin on ice. Slowly pour in warm cream, stirring until gelatin dissolves. Add milk and stir until consistency of sour cream. Pour into ramekins. Refrigerate for 24 hours.

To prepare compote, combine 1/2 cup sugar, corn syrup, vanilla bean seeds and 1 1/2 cups water in a saucepan; stir over medium heat until sugar dissolves.

Combine cherries, 1 teaspoon sugar and lemon juice. Add to the syrup. Bring to boil on medium-high heat, lower heat and simmer until reduced, 30 minutes. Cool for 5 minutes. Stir in Muscat. Refrigerate 1 hour.

To serve, place ramekins in warm water for 30 seconds; invert on plates. Drizzle with compote. Makes 6 servings.

Grapes Gelée and Yogurt Panna Cotta
Aconex

GELÉE

1 teaspoon unflavored gelatin (from a 1/4-ounce envelope)

1 cup grape juice, divided

1 tablespoon fresh lemon juice

6 ounces red and green seedless grapes, thinly sliced crosswise

1 tablespoon grappa

PANNA COTTA

2 teaspoons unflavored gelatin (from another 1/4-ounce envelope)

1 cup heavy cream, divided

1/2 cup packed dark brown sugar

2 cups low-fat plain yogurt

2 tablespoons grappa

6 8-ounce clear glasses

To prepare the gelée, sprinkle gelatin over 1/4 cup grape juice in a heavy 1-quart saucepan and let stand for 1 minute to soften. Bring to a simmer over moderate heat, stirring until gelatin is dissolved.

Remove from the heat and stir in remaining 3/4 cup grape juice, lemon juice, grapes and grappa.

Divide grape mixture among the glasses and chill in the freezer until just set, about 30 minutes.

Meanwhile, prepare the panna cotta: Stir together gelatin and 1/4 cup cream in a cleaned 1-quart heavy saucepan and let stand for 1 minute to soften. Bring to a simmer over moderate heat, stirring until gelatin is dissolved. Add remaining 3/4 cup cream and brown sugar; return to a simmer, stirring until sugar is dissolved.

Whisk together yogurt and grappa until smooth in a large measuring cup, then pour into the cream mixture and whisk until well blended.

Pour into the glasses over the set gelée and refrigerate, covered, until firm, at least 8 hours.

Serve chilled. Makes 6 servings.

Tip: Panna cotta with gelée can be chilled in glasses, covered, up to 2 days.

Glazed Apples in Caramel Sauce
Columbia Marketing International

4 large CMI* Granny Smith apples

4 tablespoons butter

4 tablespoons Amaretto liqueur or caramel syrup (the kind used for coffee flavoring)

Whipped cream or vanilla ice cream

Toasted slivered almonds, for garnish

CARAMEL SAUCE

1 cup sugar

1/2 cup water

1/2 cup light corn syrup

Salt

3/4 cup heavy cream

Preheat oven to 375°F.

Peel and core apples. Slice each apple horizontally into 5 or 6 slices, then reassemble into a stack. Place apples in a 13-by-9-inch baking dish.

Melt butter and whisk in Amaretto or caramel syrup. Drizzle over the apples.

Bake, uncovered, for about 60 minutes, or until tender to the fork. Baste every 15 minutes with the butter mixture drippings in the baking dish.

To prepare the sauce, stir together sugar, water, corn syrup and a pinch of salt in a heavy saucepan. Bring to a boil over medium heat, stirring until sugar is dissolved. Boil, without stirring, until the mixture turns a golden caramel color.

Remove from the heat and slowly stir in cream. Let cool. (Can be made ahead of time and then reheated.)

To assemble, place glazed apples on large dessert plates. Pour the warm Caramel Sauce down the center of each apple. Serve warm with a large dollop of fresh whipped cream or ice cream. Sprinkle with toasted almonds. Serve immediately.
Makes 4 servings.

Tip: Whip heavy cream with 2 tablespoons Amaretto liqueur or caramel syrup.

Recipe courtesy of Chef David Toal of Ravenous Catering, Wenatchee, Washington.
* Brands may vary by region; substitute a similar product.

Wine Poached Pears in Chocolate Sauce
California Pear Advisory Board

1 bottle (750 ml) red wine

2/3 cup sugar

2 1/4 cups cold water

1/4 cup lemon juice, plus more for coating pears

Grated peel of 1 lemon

1/2 teaspoon ground cinnamon

1/2 teaspoon ground ginger

1/2 teaspoon grated nutmeg

1 pinch ground cloves

6 California Bartlett or Bosc pears

Fat-free chocolate syrup

Chocolate shavings (optional)

In a large saucepan or Dutch oven, combine wine, sugar, water, 1/4 cup lemon juice and lemon peel. Bring to a boil and cook until reduced by 1/4. Stir in cinnamon, ginger, nutmeg and cloves.

Meanwhile, peel pears and sprinkle with lemon juice.

Stand pears in the pan with the syrup, not touching each other. Reduce heat, cover and simmer for 15 minutes. Let pears cool in the syrup, then gently lift with a slotted spoon and place on a platter or bowl. Set the red wine mixture aside.

To serve, pour chocolate syrup into individual serving bowls and warm slightly in the microwave. Place poached pears on top of chocolate and drizzle with poaching juices. Top with additional chocolate syrup or chocolate shavings. Makes 6 servings.

Tip: Pears can be poached up to two days ahead and refrigerated. Warm in the microwave or eat cold.

Crispy Coconut Rice Pudding
Kirkland Signature/Rodelle Vanilla

CRISPY COCONUT

- **1 large egg white**
- **3 tablespoons sugar**
- **1/2 teaspoon Rodelle vanilla extract**
- **Pinch of salt**
- **2 1/2 cups (4 ounces) unsweetened coconut shavings**

PUDDING

- **2 14-ounce cans light unsweetened coconut milk**
- **1 14-ounce can regular unsweetened coconut milk**
- **2/3 cup sugar**
- **2/3 cup unsweetened shredded coconut**
- **2/3 cup short- or long-grain rice (such as Arborio)**
- **3/4 teaspoon salt**
- **1 Rodelle vanilla bean**

Preheat oven to 300°F.

To prepare the crispy coconut, whisk egg white, sugar, vanilla and salt together. Add coconut shavings and stir to coat. Spread evenly on a parchment-lined baking sheet. Bake until coconut is golden and crisp, stirring frequently, about 22 minutes. Let cool.

To prepare the pudding, combine light and regular coconut milk, sugar, shredded coconut, rice and salt in a large heavy saucepan.

Split vanilla bean lengthwise and scrape out seeds; add bean and seeds to the saucepan.

Bring to a simmer over medium heat, stirring occasionally. Lower heat to barely simmering; partially cover. Cook, stirring frequently, until pudding thickens to consistency of loose oatmeal, about 45 minutes. Remove vanilla bean.

Divide among dessert glasses. Garnish with crispy coconut. Serve warm or at room temperature. Makes 10 servings.

RODELLE
A FAMILY OF FINE VANILLAS

Fruity-luscious Parfait Treat
Sun Pacific/Mas Melons & Grapes

- **1 cup small marshmallows**
- **1 cup low-fat sour cream or whipped cream**
- **6 ladyfingers, cut into small pieces**
- **1 cup sliced Mas Melons & Grapes* honeydew melon**
- **1 cup seedless grapes, sliced**
- **4 Cuties* California clementines, peeled and sectioned**
- **1/2 cup raisins**
- **1 cup graham cracker crumbs**
- **1/2 cup chopped walnuts and almonds**

Mix marshmallows with cream.

Using a clear glass dish, layer the ingredients in the following order: half of the ladyfingers, a third of the marshmallow/cream mix, half of the honeydew and grapes, a third of the clementines, and half of the raisins and graham cracker crumbs. Repeat the layering process. Top with the remaining marshmallow/cream mix and clementines.

Sprinkle with chopped walnuts and almonds. Makes 4 servings.

Brands may vary by region; substitute a similar product.

Cantaloupe and Blueberry Parfaits
Del Monte Fresh Produce

6 tablespoons nonfat lemon yogurt
$1/4$ cup fat-free sour cream
2 cups cubed Del Monte* cantaloupe

1 cup blueberries
4 mint sprigs

Mix yogurt and sour cream.

Layer $1/2$ cup cantaloupe, $1/4$ cup blueberries and $2 1/2$ tablespoons yogurt mixture in each of four 8-ounce glasses. (Stemmed glasses add an elegant touch).

Garnish with fresh mint sprigs. Makes 4 servings.

Brands may vary by region; substitute a similar product.

Fresh Fruits on a Skewer with Mixed Fruit Mousse
Ready Pac

1 4-pound Ready Pac Fruit Bowl
1 tablespoon sugar
1/2 teaspoon vanilla extract

1/4 teaspoon ground mace
3 cups whipped topping
10 10-inch bamboo skewers

In a food processor or heavy-duty blender, puree *half* of the pineapple, cantaloupe and strawberries, and *all* of the mango. Use a rubber spatula to press the fruit puree through a fine sieve to strain out any large or fibrous pieces.

Place about 2 1/2 cups of puréed fruit in a large bowl. Add sugar, vanilla and mace; mix well. Use a rubber spatula to fold whipped topping into the fruit puree until blended. Avoid overmixing. Divide the mousse equally among 8-10 chilled martini glasses, or place in a soufflé dish. Chill for 30-45 minutes.

Meanwhile, thread bamboo skewers with grapes, kiwi, cantaloupe, strawberries and pineapple. Begin and end with grapes or use them as spacers.

To serve, place skewers of fruit on dessert plates accompanied by chilled mousse. Makes 8-10 servings.

White Peach Crisp
Kingsburg Orchards

FILLING
4 large Kingsburg Orchards white peaches

1-2 teaspoons ground cinnamon

3 tablespoons brown sugar

1/2 cup water

TOPPING
1 stick (4 ounces) butter or margarine

3/4 cup flour

2/3 cup sugar

Sprinkles of brown sugar and cinnamon

Preheat oven to 375°F.

To prepare the filling, wash, peel and slice peaches. Place in a buttered 9-by-9-inch baking dish and sprinkle with cinnamon and brown sugar. Pour 1/2 cup water over peaches.

To prepare the topping, cut cold butter into the flour and sugar. (This mixture should be grainy and chunky, not smooth.) Cover the peaches with this mixture. Sprinkle with brown sugar and cinnamon to taste.

Bake for about 50 minutes, or until the topping is golden brown. Serve warm. Makes 8 servings.

Peach, Apricot and Amaretti Crisp
Pride Packing Co./Blossom Hill Packing Co.

1 tablespoon cornstarch

1 tablespoon lemon juice

1/2 teaspoon almond extract

1 1/2 pounds Mary's Pride* peaches (or nectarines), peeled and cut into 1/2-inch slices

1 1/2 pounds Blossom Hill* apricots, peeled and cut into 1/2-inch slices

1/2 cup flour

1 cup firmly packed brown sugar

3/4 cup crushed amaretti cookies (about 16 cookies)

1 teaspoon ground cinnamon

1/2 teaspoon grated nutmeg

1/8 teaspoon salt

6 tablespoons (3/4 stick) cold butter

Vanilla ice cream or heavy cream (optional)

Preheat oven to 375°F.

Whisk cornstarch, lemon juice and almond extract together.

Spread sliced peaches and apricots in a lightly buttered 2 1/2- to 3-quart baking dish. Top fruit with the cornstarch mixture.

In a bowl, stir together flour, brown sugar, amaretti, cinnamon, nutmeg, salt and butter with a pastry blender or your fingertips until the mixture forms small clumps. Spread evenly over the peaches and apricots.

Bake in the middle of the oven until the topping is golden and the fruit is tender, 35-40 minutes. Let cool slightly.

Serve warm with ice cream or a cool pitcher of heavy cream. Makes 6 servings.

Brands may vary by region; substitute a similar product.

Cherry and Blueberry Cobbler
Grower Direct Marketing/ Western Sweet Cherry Group

1 1/2 cups Grower Direct Marketing* blueberries

1 1/2 cups halved and pitted Grower Direct Marketing* fresh cherries

2/3 cup sugar

1/2 cup warm water

6 tablespoons butter

3/4 cup sugar

1 cup all-purpose flour, unsifted

1 teaspoon baking powder

1 cup milk

1 tablespoon white sugar

1 tablespoon brown sugar

Vanilla bean ice cream

Preheat oven to 350°F.

In a bowl, gently toss blueberries and cherries with 2/3 cup sugar and water; set aside.

Melt butter in an ovenproof 2-quart rectangular baking dish. In a separate bowl, combine 3/4 cup sugar, flour and baking powder. Stir in milk. Pour into the baking dish on top of the butter. Spread the fruit mixture evenly over the batter, adding 1/2 cup of the juice along with the fruit.

Mix 2 tablespoons of sugars and sprinkle over the top.

Bake for approximately 1 hour, or until the crust is done. Let cool for 30 minutes.

Serve warm with ice cream. Makes 6-8 servings.

Brands may vary by region; substitute a similar product.

Apple and Pear Crisp
Chelan Fresh

2 pounds ripe Chelan Fresh*
  Bosc pears (4 pears)
2 pounds Chelan Fresh* Granny
  Smith apples (6 apples)
1 teaspoon grated orange peel
1 teaspoon grated lemon peel
2 tablespoons freshly squeezed
  orange juice
2 tablespoons freshly squeezed
  lemon juice
1/2 cup granulated sugar
1/4 cup all-purpose flour
1 teaspoon ground cinnamon
1/2 teaspoon ground nutmeg

TOPPING

1 1/2 cups all-purpose flour
3/4 cup granulated sugar
3/4 cup lightly packed light
  brown sugar
1/2 teaspoon salt
1 cup old-fashioned oatmeal
1/2 pound (2 sticks) cold unsalted
  butter, diced

Preheat oven to 350°F.

To prepare the topping, combine all ingredients in the bowl of an electric mixer fitted with the paddle attachment. Mix on low speed for 1 minute, until the mixture is in large crumbles.

Peel, core and cut pears and apples into large chunks. Place the fruit in a large bowl and add grated orange and lemon peel, orange and lemon juice, sugar, flour, cinnamon and nutmeg. Stir to coat. Pour into a 9-by-12-by-2-inch baking dish. Sprinkle the topping evenly over the fruit, covering the fruit completely.

Place the baking dish on a sheet pan and bake for 50-60 minutes, or until the top is brown and the fruit is bubbly. Serve warm. Makes 8 servings.

Brands may vary by region; substitute a similar product.

Plum Tart
WesPak

CRUST
1 2/3 cups flour
1/4 teaspoon salt
11 tablespoons butter,
    cut into pieces
3 tablespoons sour cream

CUSTARD
1 1/3 cups sugar
1/3 cup flour
1/4 teaspoon salt
4 large eggs
1/2 cup sour cream
7 large WesPak plums, thinly
    sliced (about 6 1/2 cups)

Preheat oven to 375°F.

To prepare the crust, pulse flour, salt and butter in a food processor until crumbly. Add sour cream. Process until it forms a ball. Press the dough into a 12-inch tart pan with a removable bottom. Bake for 18 minutes, or until lightly browned. Let cool for 15 minutes.

Reduce oven heat to 350°F.

To prepare the custard, mix sugar, flour and salt. In another bowl, beat eggs and sour cream. Add the sugar mixture to the egg mixture and blend well.

Arrange sliced plums in concentric circles on the baked crust. Gently pour the custard over the plums.

Bake for 40-50 minutes, or until the custard is set and golden brown. Let cool for 10 minutes.

Set the tart on a glass plate and gently remove the pan ring. Makes 8-12 servings.

In The Kitchen The Costco Way

Persimmon Tarts
Aconex

2 puff pastry sheets

1 egg yolk

2 persimmons, peeled and cut in thin slices

2 tablespoons apricot jelly, melted

4 mint leaves

PASTRY CREAM

2 cups whole milk

Zest of 1 orange, removed with a vegetable peeler

Zest of 1 lemon, removed with a vegetable peeler

1 vanilla bean

5 large egg yolks

1/2 cup sugar

6 tablespoons all-purpose flour

2 tablespoons unsalted butter

To prepare the pastry cream, place milk, orange and lemon zest, and vanilla bean in a medium saucepan. Bring to a boil over medium-high heat. Remove from the heat, cover and let cool for 5 minutes. Strain the milk into a bowl.

Whisk egg yolks, sugar and flour in a medium bowl to blend. Gradually whisk in milk. Return to the saucepan and cook over medium heat, whisking constantly, until the pastry cream thickens and boils, about 5 minutes. Whisk in butter.

Transfer the pastry cream to a bowl. Press plastic wrap onto the surface. Chill until cold, at least 4 hours and up to 1 day.

Preheat oven to 350°F.

Roll out puff pastry sheets to 1/4-inch thickness. Cut 8 circles with a round 3 1/2-inch cookie-cutter. Cut a hole in the center of 4 circles, forming a ring. Brush the edges of the 4 solid circles with water. Place the rings on top and press slightly; prick the center with a fork. Combine egg yolk with 1 tablespoon water and brush on the edges of the rings.

Bake pastry for 20-30 minutes, or until golden. Let cool on a rack.

Fill the puff pastry molds with pastry cream. Lay persimmon slices over the pastry cream. Brush apricot jelly on top and garnish with mint leaves. Makes 4 servings.

Seedless Grape and Fruit Pizza
Pandol Bros., Inc.

CRUST
- 1 packaged lemon cake mix
- 2/3 cup graham cracker crumbs
- 1/2 cup chopped walnuts (optional)
- 1/2 cup butter, softened
- 1 egg

TOPPING
- 3 ounces cream cheese
- 1/3 cup granulated sugar
- 1 cup whipping cream
- 2 cups Pandol red seedless grapes, halved
- 2 cups Pandol green seedless grapes, halved
- 1/2 pound strawberries, cut into bite-size pieces
- 2 cups blackberries or 1 cup blueberries
- 3 tablespoons grape jelly

Preheat oven to 350°F.

To prepare the crust, combine cake mix, graham cracker crumbs, walnuts and butter. Mix until crumbly. Blend in egg.

Press into an ungreased 12- to 14-inch pizza pan. Bake for 15 minutes, or until golden brown. Let cool.

To prepare the topping, whip cream cheese until fluffy. Gradually add sugar, blending well. Beat in whipping cream until soft peaks form.

Spread topping over the crust. Arrange fruit on top.

Melt jelly and drizzle over the fruit.

Serve immediately or chill for later use. Makes 8-10 servings.

Recipe developed by Sherry Wysinger, Pandol Bros., Inc. employee.

Raisin Peach Cobbler
Sun-Maid Growers

- 1 1/4 cups sugar, divided
- 1 cup all-purpose flour
- 1 1/2 teaspoons baking powder
- 1/4 teaspoon salt
- 1 cup milk
- 1/2 cup butter or margarine, melted
- 2 cups peeled peach slices, fresh, frozen or canned
- 1 cup Sun-Maid raisins
- 1 teaspoon ground cinnamon
- 1/4 teaspoon grated nutmeg
- 1/4 teaspoon ground allspice
- Ice cream (optional)

Heat oven to 350°F. Grease a 9-inch square pan.

In a large bowl, combine 1 cup sugar, flour, baking powder and salt; mix well. Blend in milk and butter. Pour the batter into the greased pan.

Combine peaches, raisins, remaining 1/4 cup sugar, cinnamon, nutmeg and allspice; toss to coat evenly. Spoon the peach mixture evenly over the batter.

Bake for 45 minutes, or until lightly browned.

Serve warm or at room temperature with ice cream, if desired. Makes 6 servings.

Lemon Tarts with Mascarpone Cream and Blackberries
Give & Go Prepared Foods

MASCARPONE CREAM

8 ounces chilled mascarpone cheese

¹/₂ cup chilled heavy cream

¹/₂ cup confectioners' sugar

1 teaspoon vanilla extract

1 tablespoon crème de cassis liqueur (or blackberry-flavored liqueur)

4 5-inch Kirkland Signature lemon *or* strawberry/blueberry tarts

2 cups blackberries, rinsed

To prepare the Mascarpone Cream, place mascarpone, heavy cream, confectioners' sugar, vanilla and cassis in a large bowl. Blend with an electric mixer on high for 3-4 minutes, or until smooth. Chill in the refrigerator.

Cut the tarts in half. Place each half on a rectangular or oblong glass plate.

Place 1 ¹/₂ tablespoons of Mascarpone Cream on either side of the tart.

Top Mascarpone Cream with a few blackberries and place a few blackberries randomly around the plate. Makes 8 servings.

GIVE & GO®

No-Bake S'more Pie
J&J Snack Foods

*CHOCOLATE
COOKIE CRUST*

1 1/2 cups crumbled Kirkland
  Signature chocolate
  chunk cookies

2-3 tablespoons
  granulated sugar

1/4 cup butter

FILLING

3 cups miniature
  marshmallows

1/2 cup light cream

1 cup dairy whipped cream

1 dark milk chocolate
  candy bar

1/4 cup graham
  cracker crumbs

To prepare the crust, combine all ingredients in a 9-inch glass pie plate. Heat on high in the microwave for 2 minutes, stirring once. Press evenly onto the bottom and sides of the dish. Heat on high for 1 minute to set the crust. (This can be made in advance and frozen.)

To prepare the filling, combine marshmallows and cream in a 2-quart glass bowl. Microwave on high for 2-2 1/2 minutes, or until marshmallows puff. Stir well to blend evenly. Chill for 20-25 minutes, or until thickened but not set.

Fold in whipped cream. Pour into the crust. Top with shavings from the candy bar and graham cracker crumbs. Chill for 4-5 hours before serving. Makes 6-8 servings.

Chocolate Crumb Cream Pie
Barry Callebaut

1/2 cup plus 1 quart
  milk, divided

1 1/2 tablespoons gelatin

1 1/2 cups sugar, divided

3/4 cup cornstarch

4 ounces Callebaut
  unsweetened
  baking chocolate

5 egg yolks

1/4 teaspoon salt

1 tablespoon vanilla
  extract

1 cup whipped cream

2 prebaked 9-inch
  pie shells

Callebaut semisweet
  chocolate shavings,
  for garnish

2 large Kirkland Signature
  chocolate chip cookies,
  crumbled, for garnish

Combine 1/2 cup milk and gelatin; set aside.

Place 1 quart milk and 3/4 cup sugar in a saucepan and bring to a boil.

Combine the remaining 3/4 cup sugar and cornstarch, using some of the milk to form a paste. Whisk into the boiling milk.

Add unsweetened chocolate and stir until it melts.

Place egg yolks in a bowl and whisk. Whisk in a little of the hot chocolate mixture and then stir eggs into the saucepan. Remove from the heat and let sit for 3 minutes.

Stir the gelatin mixture into the chocolate mixture.

Pour into a bowl that is placed on a bed of ice. Stir in salt and continue stirring until completely cool.

Add vanilla. Fold in whipped cream.

Fill the pie shells with the mixture. Decorate with chocolate shavings and crumbled cookies. Makes 20 servings.

CALLEBAUT
INSPIRED BY YOUR CRAFTSMANSHIP

Vanilla Almond Bars
Banana Coconut Pie
Häagen-Dazs

1 cup heavy cream
1/4 cup granulated sugar
2 bananas, sliced
1 teaspoon lemon juice
3/4 cup sweetened flaked coconut, toasted
1 purchased 8-inch graham cracker or vanilla wafer crumb piecrust (6 ounces)
6 Häagen-Dazs Vanilla & Almond Bars (3 ounces each)

In a medium bowl, beat cream and sugar to firm peaks.

In a separate bowl, combine bananas and lemon juice; mash gently, leaving some of the banana in small pieces.

Set aside 2 tablespoons toasted coconut for garnish. Fold remaining coconut and bananas into the cream. Spread the mixture evenly in the crust.

Unwrap and gently remove sticks from Vanilla & Almond Bars. Press the long edge of the bars about halfway into the cream, arranging them on the pie in a pinwheel pattern.

Sprinkle reserved coconut between the bars.

Cover the pie lightly with plastic wrap and freeze for 6-8 hours, or until firm.

Remove from the freezer 10 minutes before serving. Cut into slices. Makes 6 servings.

Tip: To toast coconut, spread evenly in a glass pie dish. Microwave for 1 minute on high; stir. Repeat microwaving and stirring at 30-second intervals until coconut is lightly browned. Watch carefully, as spots may burn.

Chocolate Peanut Butter
Mousse Pie
Eagle Brand/Jif

1 14-ounce can Eagle Brand* sweetened condensed milk, divided
2/3 cup semisweet chocolate chips
1 9-inch graham cracker crust
1 8-ounce package cream cheese, softened
1 cup Jif* Creamy Peanut Butter
2 cups frozen whipped dessert topping, thawed

Combine 1/3 cup sweetened condensed milk and chocolate chips in a microwave-safe bowl. Microwave on high for 30 seconds. Stir until smooth. Place 2 tablespoons of the chocolate mixture in a resealable plastic bag for drizzle; set aside. Spread remaining chocolate evenly over the bottom of the piecrust. Chill for 10 minutes.

In a large bowl, beat remaining sweetened condensed milk, cream cheese and peanut butter with an electric mixer until smooth. Fold in topping. Spoon over the chocolate layer.

Cut a corner off the bag with reserved chocolate. Drizzle over the pie.

Freeze for 1 hour, or until firm. Makes 8-10 servings.

Tip: The pie can be made ahead and kept in the freezer. Refrigerate for 30-45 minutes before serving.

Brands may vary by region; substitute a similar product.

Chocolate Silk Pie
Land O' Lakes

CRUST

1 ½ cups (about 18) finely crushed
chocolate sandwich cookies

¼ cup Land O Lakes*
butter, melted

FILLING

1 cup sugar

¾ cup Land O Lakes*
butter, slightly softened

3 1-ounce squares semisweet
baking chocolate, melted, cooled

¾ cup refrigerated
egg substitute

GARNISH

Land O Lakes* Aerosol Whipped
Heavy Cream or Land O Lakes*
Aerosol Whipped
Light Cream

Chocolate curls (optional)

To prepare the crust, stir together all ingredients in a medium bowl. Press onto the bottom and sides of a 9-inch pie pan. Refrigerate for 10 minutes.

To prepare the filling, combine sugar and butter in a small bowl. Beat at medium speed, scraping the bowl often, until well mixed. Add melted chocolate and continue beating, scraping the bowl often, until well mixed. Add egg substitute and beat until light and fluffy.

Spoon the filling into the crust. Refrigerate for at least 3 hours, or until set.

Garnish with whipped cream and chocolate curls, if desired. Store in the refrigerator. Makes 8 servings.

Brands may vary by region; substitute a similar product.

Where simple goodness begins.®

Dutch Apple Pie
Oneonta Starr Ranch Growers

FILLING

6-8 Oneonta Starr Ranch Growers apples (Fuji, Golden Delicious or a mixture)

1 cup sugar

1/4 cup flour

1/2 teaspoon ground cinnamon

1/8 teaspoon freshly grated nutmeg

1 teaspoon lemon juice

CRUST

1 stick (1/2 cup) butter

8 ounces cream cheese

2 1/2 cups flour

1/2 teaspoon salt

1/2 cup cold water

TOPPING

1/2 cup flour

1/4 cup packed brown sugar

1/4 cup sugar

1/2 stick (1/4 cup) butter

1 teaspoon ground cinnamon

Preheat oven to 350°F.

To prepare the filling, peel, core and thinly slice apples. Mix all ingredients together and set aside.

To prepare the crust, place butter, cream cheese, flour and salt in a food processor; pulse until pea size. Add water a little at a time, just until blended. Form the dough into 2 balls, making one a little bigger. Roll out the larger ball of dough, place in a 9-inch pie pan, trim and crimp edges. (Use remaining dough for another recipe.)

To prepare the topping, blend all ingredients until pea size.

Fill the piecrust with filling. Spread topping over the apples.

Bake for 1 hour, or until the topping is golden. Makes 8 servings.

Recipe by Stacey Sarty, Director of Growing and Orchard Operations, Grand Champion Winner of the Apple Blossom Festival (2006), Wenatchee, Washington (Apple Capital of the World).

Apple Cranberry Pie
Splenda

1 15-ounce package refrigerated piecrusts

1/2 cup Splenda No Calorie Sweetener, granulated

1 tablespoon all-purpose flour

1/2 teaspoon ground cinnamon

4 large Granny Smith apples, peeled, cored and sliced

1 cup cranberries, coarsely chopped

Preheat oven to 400°F.

Unfold 1 piecrust; press out fold lines. Fit into a 9-inch pie pan according to package directions.

Combine Splenda, flour and cinnamon in a large bowl; add apples and cranberries, tossing gently. Spoon the mixture into the piecrust.

Unfold remaining piecrust; press out fold lines. Roll to 1/8-inch thickness. Place over the filling; fold edges under and crimp. Cut slits in the top to allow steam to escape.

Bake for 40-50 minutes, or until the crust is golden. Cover edges with aluminum foil to prevent over-browning, if necessary. Cool on a wire rack for 1 hour before serving. Makes 8 servings.

Bread Pudding with Chocolate-Covered Raisins
Kirkland Signature/Kerry

Butter, melted

3 1/2 cups chopped croissant, cinnamon roll or bread pieces

1/4 cup brown sugar

1 teaspoon ground cinnamon

1 1/2 cups Kirkland Signature chocolate-covered raisins

6 large eggs, beaten

1/2 cup granulated sugar

1 teaspoon vanilla extract

1/4 teaspoon grated nutmeg

2 1/2 cups heavy cream

2 1/2 cups 2% milk

1/4 cup apricot preserves (optional)

Whipped cream (optional)

Preheat oven to 325°F. Brush an 8-by-8-inch pan with melted butter.

Place croissant, cinnamon roll or bread pieces in the pan. Sprinkle with brown sugar and cinnamon and toss lightly, then sprinkle with chocolate-covered raisins.

In a separate bowl, mix beaten eggs with granulated sugar, vanilla, nutmeg, heavy cream and milk. Pour the mixture over the ingredients in the pan.

Bake for 1-1 1/4 hours, or until set. It should still jiggle.

Brush with apricot preserves to glaze when hot from the oven.

Serve hot or cold. Top with whipped cream if desired. Makes 8 servings.

Tip: For a lighter version, use regular bread, nonfat milk and egg substitute.

Bing Cherry and Chocolate Streusel Bread Pudding
L&M Companies

Butter-flavored
    cooking spray
5 large eggs
4 large egg whites
1 1/4 cups skim milk
1/2 cup white sugar
1 tablespoon vanilla extract
1/2 teaspoon ground
    cinnamon
1/2 teaspoon grated nutmeg
1/2 teaspoon ground allspice
5 cups 1-inch cubes
    whole-grain bread
    with crusts removed
3 cups fresh Jubilee
    Cherries* Bing cherries:
    1/2 pitted and diced,
    1/2 reserved whole
3/4 cup mini milk-
    chocolate chips
1/4 cup finely chopped
    pecans or walnuts
6 ounces milk
    chocolate, melted
Whipped cream

STREUSEL
1/3 cup flour
1/4 cup oatmeal
2 tablespoons
    chopped pecans
3 tablespoons brown sugar
2 tablespoons butter,
    softened

Preheat oven to 375°F. Coat a 13-by-9-inch glass pan with cooking spray.

In a bowl, whisk together eggs, egg whites and milk. Add sugar, vanilla and spices, blending well.

In another bowl, toss bread cubes, diced cherries, chocolate chips and nuts. Pour in the egg mixture and stir until well coated.

Press firmly into the greased baking dish and cover with foil. Bake until the custard is set, 40-45 minutes.

To prepare the streusel, combine all ingredients in a small bowl and stir to blend.

Remove the foil and sprinkle the pudding with streusel. Bake, uncovered, until puffed and golden brown, 15-20 minutes longer. Let cool for 15-20 minutes before serving.

To serve, drizzle melted milk chocolate over the pudding and top with cold whipped cream and the reserved whole cherries. Makes 12 servings.

* Brands may vary by region; substitute a similar product.

Cherry Blossoms
Cherry Central

2/3 cup sifted
    confectioners' sugar
1/4 cup heavy cream
    or milk
1 cup Cherry Central*
    dried tart
    cherries, divided
1/4 cup coarsely
    chopped pecans
1 14- to 16-ounce loaf
    frozen white bread
    dough, thawed
2 tablespoons butter or
    margarine, melted
1/4 cup brown sugar
1 1/2 teaspoons ground
    cinnamon

In a small bowl, combine confectioners' sugar and cream or milk; mix well. Pour into a 9-inch deep-dish pie pan. Sprinkle evenly with 1/2 cup cherries and pecans.

On a lightly floured surface, roll bread dough into a 12-by-8-inch rectangle; brush with melted butter.

In a small bowl, combine brown sugar and cinnamon; sprinkle over the dough. Top with remaining 1/2 cup cherries. Roll up the dough, jelly-roll style, starting from the long side; pinch to seal the edges. Cut the roll into 12 slices.

Place the slices, cut side down, in the pan. Cover and let rise in a warm place for 30 minutes, or until doubled.

Preheat oven to 375°F.

Bake the rolls, uncovered, for 20-25 minutes, or until golden brown. Cover with foil during the last 10 minutes to prevent overbrowning. Let cool in the pan for 1-2 minutes, then invert onto a serving platter. Serve warm. Makes 12 rolls.

* Brands may vary by region; substitute a similar product.

Cherry Central

Orange Dream Chiffon Cake
Seald Sweet

5 Seald Sweet Navel or
   Valencia oranges
2 1/4 cups cake flour
1 tablespoon baking
   powder
3/4 teaspoon salt
1 3/4 cups granulated
   sugar, divided
1/2 cup vegetable oil
5 large eggs, separated
2 large egg whites
1/2 teaspoon cream
   of tartar
1 cup heavy cream

Preheat oven to 325°F.

Reserve 1 orange for garnish. From other oranges, grate 3 tablespoons peel and squeeze 1 cup juice.

In a large bowl, stir together flour, baking powder, salt and 1 cup sugar. Make a well in the center. Add oil, egg yolks, 1 tablespoon orange peel and 3/4 cup orange juice; whisk into dry ingredients.

In another large bowl, beat on high speed 7 egg whites and cream of tartar until soft peaks form. Sprinkle in 1/2 cup sugar, 2 spoonfuls at a time, and beat until the whites peak. Gently fold into batter. Pour into an ungreased 10-inch angel food cake pan.

Bake for 60-65 minutes, or until the top springs back when touched. Invert cake and cool completely, about 2 hours. Remove from the pan.

Beat cream on high speed, slowly adding 1/4 cup sugar, 1/4 cup orange juice and 2 tablespoons grated peel. Spoon frosting over cake. Garnish with orange segments. Makes 10-12 servings.

Seald Sweet
INTERNATIONAL

Chocolate Cake with Berries and Chocolate Shavings
Kirkland Signature

2 tablespoons
   chocolate syrup
1 3-by-3-inch slice
   Kirkland Signature
   filled half-sheet
   chocolate cake
3 raspberries
2 blackberries
1 ounce milk chocolate
   (e.g., Hershey's
   Symphony bar)

Drizzle chocolate syrup onto a plate.

Place cake slice on the plate. Arrange berries next to the cake.

Using a potato peeler, shave milk chocolate strips onto the cake and berries. Makes 1 serving.

Tip: Blueberries and strawberries can also be used.

Apple Pear Cake
Kingsburg Orchards

CAKE
3 cups flour
1 teaspoon salt
1 teaspoon baking soda
2 teaspoons ground cinnamon
1 cup white sugar
1 cup packed brown sugar
3 large eggs, beaten
3/4 cup milk
2 teaspoons vanilla extract
4 cups diced Kingsburg Orchards apple pears

TOPPING
1/2 cup packed brown sugar
1/4 cup milk
1/4 pound butter

Preheat oven to 350°F.

In a medium bowl, combine flour, salt, baking soda and cinnamon. Set aside.

Place white sugar and brown sugar in a large bowl. Add eggs and stir by hand until well blended. Stir in milk and vanilla.

Add the flour mixture and stir just until blended. Fold in apple pears.

Pour the batter into a greased 13-by-9-inch pan.

Bake for 45 minutes, or until a toothpick inserted in the center comes out clean.

To prepare the topping, mix all ingredients in a saucepan and cook at a slow boil for 3 minutes.

Pour the topping over the cake and return to the oven for 4 minutes, or until the topping is bubbling and golden. Makes 8 servings.

Chocolate-Raspberry Rugala Cheesecake
Countryside Baking

Nonstick cooking spray

20 pieces Kirkland Signature* Chocolate/Raspberry Rugala

32 ounces cream cheese, softened

1 cup sugar

2 teaspoons vanilla extract

4 eggs, room temperature

Raspberry preserves (optional)

Chocolate syrup (optional)

Preheat oven to 300°F. Coat a 9-inch springform pan with cooking spray and line the bottom of the pan with waxed paper.

Arrange 1 layer of 10 rugala in the pan.

In a bowl, beat cream cheese, sugar and vanilla on medium speed until smooth. On low speed, add eggs one at a time, blending well after each addition.

Pour half of the cream cheese mixture into the pan. Top with another layer of 10 rugala, and then pour in the remaining cream cheese mixture.

Set the pan in a water bath and bake for 60 minutes, or until the cake is set in the center. Let cool to room temperature, then refrigerate for about 5 hours or overnight. Use raspberry preserves and chocolate syrup to make a design on top of the cake. Makes 12 servings.

Brands may vary by region; substitute a similar product.

A DAWN FOOD PRODUCTS COMPANY

Raspberry White Chocolate Cheesecake
Raskas

1 8 1/2-ounce package chocolate wafer cookies, crushed

3 tablespoons butter, melted

8 ounces white chocolate, broken into pieces

1 1/2 pounds Raskas* cream cheese, softened

1 cup sugar

4 eggs

1 tablespoon vanilla extract

2 cups whipping cream, divided

2/3 cup raspberry jam

1/2 cup ground walnuts

Preheat oven to 325°F.

Mix cookie crumbs and butter. Press onto the bottom and partway up the sides of a 9-inch springform pan. Arrange chocolate pieces over the crust.

Place cream cheese and sugar in a mixer bowl and beat until blended. Add eggs one at a time, beating well after each addition. Add vanilla and 1 1/2 cups whipping cream. Beat at medium speed for 10 minutes.

Spoon 2/3 of the cream cheese mixture over the chocolate. Drop spoonfuls of jam on the mixture. Top with the remaining cream cheese mixture. Swirl a knife gently through the jam and cream cheese mixture for a marbling effect.

Bake for 1 1/2 hours, or until set. Let cool, then refrigerate until chilled.

To serve, whip 1/2 cup cream. Pipe a border around the edges of the cake. Sprinkle with walnuts. Makes 8-12 servings.

Brands may vary by region; substitute a similar product.

SCHREIBER™

Three Berry Cheesecake with Chocolate-Dipped Strawberries
Kirkland Signature

20 large fresh strawberries
1 pint heavy whipping cream
2 tablespoons confectioners' sugar
1 teaspoon vanilla extract
1 Kirkland Signature* Three Berry Cheesecake (or any other Kirkland Signature cheesecake)
Large sprig of mint, for garnish

SEMISWEET DIPPING CHOCOLATE
1 cup semisweet chocolate chips
1 tablespoon shortening

WHITE DIPPING CHOCOLATE
1/4 cup white chocolate chips
3/4 teaspoon shortening

Gently rinse strawberries and set out to dry completely, blotting with paper towels. Line a baking sheet with waxed paper.

To prepare dipping chocolate, place semisweet chocolate and shortening in a bowl and heat in the microwave 30 seconds at a time, stirring, until it is smooth (110°F). Repeat the process with white chocolate and shortening.

Dip each strawberry in semisweet chocolate and set on the waxed paper.

Fill a small sandwich bag or pastry bag with the melted white chocolate. Cut a very small hole in the bag and pipe white-chocolate decorations onto the strawberries.

Whip cream on high speed until soft peaks form. Add confectioners' sugar and vanilla. Continue beating for another 30 seconds.

Using a large spatula, carefully lift the cheesecake off the plate and onto a cake stand. Lay the chocolate-dipped strawberries in a ring around the cake, with the stems facing out. Place a large dollop of whipped cream in the center and garnish with fresh mint. Serve remaining whipped cream on the side. Makes 16 servings.

Brands may vary by region; substitute a similar product.

German Raw Apple Cake
Holtzinger Fruit

2 1/4 cups flour
2 large eggs
1/2 cup brown sugar
1 cup white sugar
1/4 teaspoon salt
2 teaspoons baking soda
2 teaspoons ground cinnamon
1/2 cup shortening
1 cup sour milk (1 tablespoon
   vinegar + 1 cup milk)

2 cups peeled and thinly sliced
   Holtzinger Fruit* apples
   (Granny Smith, Jonagold or
   Golden Delicious)

TOPPING
1/4 cup brown sugar
1/4 cup white sugar
1/2 teaspoon ground cinnamon
1/2 cup chopped nuts

Preheat oven to 350°F.

In a large mixing bowl, combine flour, eggs, brown sugar, white sugar, salt, baking soda, cinnamon, shortening and sour milk. Mix until well blended. Fold in apples.

Pour the batter into a greased 12-by-9-inch cake pan.

To prepare the topping, combine all ingredients and mix to blend. Sprinkle over the cake batter.

Bake for 45 minutes, or until a toothpick inserted in the center comes out clean. Makes 12 servings.

* Brands may vary by region; substitute a similar product.

Best Ever Peanut Butter-Oatmeal Cookies
Skippy

2 cups quick-cooking oats

2 cups all-purpose flour

1 teaspoon baking powder

1 teaspoon baking soda

1/4 teaspoon salt

1 cup Shedd's Spread* Country Crock Spread

1 cup Skippy* Creamy or Super Chunk Peanut Butter

1 cup granulated sugar

1 cup firmly packed brown sugar

2 eggs

2 teaspoons vanilla extract

1 12-ounce package semi-sweet chocolate chips (optional)

Preheat oven to 350°F.

In a small bowl, combine oats, flour, baking powder, baking soda and salt; set aside.

In a large bowl, with an electric mixer on medium speed, beat spread and peanut butter until smooth. Beat in sugars, then eggs and vanilla until blended. Beat in flour mixture just until blended. Stir in chocolate chips.

On ungreased baking sheets, drop dough by rounded tablespoonfuls, 2 inches apart.

Bake for 13 minutes, or until golden. Remove the cookies to a wire rack and let cool completely. Makes 6 dozen cookies.

Brands may vary by region; substitute a similar product.

Easy Oreo Truffles
Kraft Foods

1 18-ounce package Oreo Chocolate Sandwich Cookies, finely crushed, divided

8 ounces Philadelphia cream cheese, softened

2 8-ounce packages semisweet baking chocolate, melted

Line a baking sheet with waxed paper.

Mix 3 cups of the cookie crumbs and cream cheese until well blended. Shape into 42 one-inch balls.

Dip balls in melted chocolate; place on the baking sheet. Sprinkle with remaining cookie crumbs. (Any leftover melted chocolate can be stored in a tightly covered container at room temperature and saved for another use.)

Refrigerate for 1 hour, or until firm. Store any leftover truffles in a tightly covered container in the refrigerator. Makes 42 truffles.

Apple Gouda Ladder Loaf
Sage Fruit

2 3-ounce packages cream cheese, divided
¹/₄ cup margarine
2 cups biscuit mix
¹/₃ cup milk
¹/₄ cup water
1 ¹/₂ teaspoons cornstarch
2 Sage Fruit Jonagold apples, peeled and thinly sliced
1 ¹/₄ teaspoons ground cinnamon
¹/₄ cup sugar
¹/₃ cup chopped pecans
2 cups grated Gouda cheese

FROSTING
1 teaspoon margarine, softened
³/₄ cup confectioners' sugar
¹/₄ teaspoon vanilla extract
2 ¹/₂ teaspoons milk

Cut 3 ounces cream cheese and margarine into biscuit mix until crumbly. Stir in milk. Knead dough 15 strokes. Roll into a 14-by-10-inch rectangle between 2 sheets waxed paper. Place dough on a greased baking sheet. Make 3-inch-long cuts at 1-inch intervals along long sides of dough.

Combine water and cornstarch in a frying pan. Stir in apples, cinnamon and sugar. Cook, stirring, for 5 minutes, or until thickened and apples begin to soften. Cool.

To prepare the frosting, blend all ingredients.

Preheat oven to 425°F.

To assemble, spread 3 ounces cream cheese on center of dough. Top with apples. Sprinkle with all but 2 tablespoons pecans. Top with Gouda. Fold strips over the filling.

Bake for 15 minutes, or until golden brown.

Cool. Drizzle with frosting. Sprinkle with reserved pecans. Makes 8 servings.

Blueberry and Tart Cherry Cream Cheese Puffs
Meduri Farms

4 ounces cream cheese, softened
¹/₄ cup confectioners' sugar
1 cup Meduri Farms* dried red sour cherries
¹/₂ cup Kirkland Signature dried blueberries
¹/₂ cup chopped pecans
1 16-ounce package refrigerated biscuits such as Pillsbury Grands Homestyle Biscuits

ICING
¹/₂ cup confectioners' sugar
2-3 teaspoons milk

Preheat oven to 350°F.

Blend cream cheese and confectioners' sugar in a medium bowl. Fold in cherries, blueberries and pecans.

Separate each biscuit evenly into 2 rounds. Press out 8 biscuit rounds on an ungreased cookie sheet until each is double in size. Drop 1 heaping tablespoon of the cream cheese mixture onto each round.

Press out 8 remaining biscuit rounds and place on top of the filled rounds. Press the edges with a fork to shape and seal the puffs.

Bake for 15-20 minutes, or until golden brown.

To prepare the icing, blend confectioners' sugar with enough milk so the icing can be drizzled on the puffs.

Remove the puffs from the oven. Place on a baking rack to cool.

Drizzle icing over the puffs while they are still warm. Serve at room temperature. Makes 8 servings.

Brands may vary by region; substitute a similar product.

Coffee Pumpkin Bread with Coffee Icing
Starbucks Coffee

1 14-ounce package pumpkin quick bread mix

1 ¼ cups brewed double-strength Starbucks coffee, any variety, cooled, divided

4 squares (4 ounces) semisweet baking chocolate, coarsely chopped

3 cups confectioners' sugar

2 tablespoons butter or margarine, melted

Prepare bread batter as directed on the package, substituting 1 cup of the coffee for the water. Stir in chocolate.

Bake bread as directed on the package. Remove from the pan; cool completely.

Beat sugar, remaining ¼ cup coffee and butter in a large bowl with an electric mixer on low speed until well blended. Spread on the bread. Makes 16 servings.

Lemon Gingerbread Bars
Kirkland Signature/Jelly Belly

GINGERBREAD
1/3 cup molasses

1/4 cup packed
   brown sugar

2 tablespoons shortening

3 tablespoons cold water

1 3/4 cups all-purpose flour

1/2 teaspoon baking soda

1 1/4 teaspoons pumpkin
   pie spice

1/4 teaspoon salt

LEMON FILLING
1 cup granulated sugar

1 tablespoon grated
   lemon peel

3 tablespoons lemon juice

1/4 teaspoon
   baking powder

1/4 teaspoon salt

3 large eggs

Confectioners' sugar

5 ounces Jelly Belly jelly
   beans in holiday colors

Preheat oven to 350°F. Grease a 13-by-9-by-2-inch pan.

To prepare the gingerbread, stir together molasses, brown sugar and shortening in a large bowl. Stir in cold water. Blend in flour, baking soda, spice and salt. Press dough onto the bottom and 1/4 inch up the sides of the pan. Bake for 10 minutes.

Meanwhile, prepare the filling. In a bowl, beat sugar, lemon peel, lemon juice, baking powder, salt and eggs with a wire whisk for about 1 minute, or until well mixed. Pour over the hot crust. Bake for 20-25 minutes, or until set.

Let cool completely. Sprinkle with confectioners' sugar. Cut bars into 6 rows by 4 rows. Decorate with jelly beans, gently pressing into the filling. Makes 24 bars.

Tiramisu Cheesecake Bars
General Mills

BASE
1 pouch Betty Crocker
   sugar cookie mix

2 tablespoons Gold Medal
   all-purpose flour

1/3 cup butter or
   margarine, softened

1 egg, slightly beaten

FILLING
2 8-ounce packages
   cream cheese, softened

1 14-ounce can sweet-
   ened condensed milk
   (not evaporated)

1 tablespoon instant coffee

2 teaspoons vanilla
   extract

2 eggs

1 cup miniature semi-
   sweet chocolate chips

TOPPING
6 ounces cream cheese,
   softened

1/2 cup whipping cream

Chocolate curls (optional)

Preheat oven to 350°F. Coat a 13-by-9-inch pan with cooking spray.

To prepare the base, combine ingredients and stir until a soft dough forms. Press into bottom of pan. Bake for 15-18 minutes, or until light golden brown. Let cool.

To prepare the filling, in another bowl, beat cream cheese until smooth. Add condensed milk; beat until blended. Beat in coffee, vanilla and eggs. Stir in chocolate chips. Pour over cookie base. Bake for 35-40 minutes, or until set. Let cool for 30 minutes. Refrigerate for 30 minutes to cool completely.

To prepare the topping, beat cream cheese on medium speed until smooth. Gradually beat in whipping cream; beat 2 minutes longer, or until fluffy. Spread over cooled bars. Refrigerate for 2 hours. Garnish with chocolate curls. Makes 36 bars.

Brownie Bite S'more
Sugar Bowl Bakery

1 teaspoon butter
1 teaspoon sugar
1 tablespoon graham cracker crumbs
1 2 1/2-by-2 1/2-inch square cutter
5 Sugar Bowl Bakery Brownie Bites*

3 large marshmallows
1 teaspoon melted milk chocolate
1 chocolate cigar

Preheat oven to 350°F.

Melt butter in an ovenproof pan. Stir in sugar and graham cracker crumbs. Bake for 10 minutes. Let the mixture cool to the touch.

Press graham cracker mixture into the square cutter.

Mash brownies and place on top of the graham cracker layer.

Place marshmallows on a skewer and heat until melted over an open flame. Remove from skewer, then set on top of the brownie layer, drizzle with chocolate and add the cigar.

Remove the s'more from the cutter and serve immediately. Makes 1 serving.

* Brands may vary by region; substitute a similar product.

Beverages

Strawberry Banana Smoothie
Equal

2 cups nonfat plain yogurt
1 medium-size ripe banana
12 packets Equal sweetener
3 tablespoons lemon juice
3 cups frozen unsweetened whole strawberries

Combine yogurt, banana, Equal and lemon juice in a blender or food processor; cover.

With the blender running, add strawberries, a few at a time, through the opening in the lid. Process until smooth.

Pour into glasses. Serve immediately. Makes 4 servings.

Orange Lemonade
Sunkist Growers

1 cup fresh-squeezed Sunkist* lemon juice
3 cups water
$1/2$ cup sugar
2 cups fresh-squeezed Sunkist* orange juice
4 Sunkist* fresh orange slices, $1/2$ inch thick
4 Sunkist* fresh lemon slices, $1/4$ inch thick
Ice cubes

In a large pitcher, combine lemon juice, water and sugar. Blend well to dissolve sugar.

Add orange juice. Mix well and chill.

Place 1 orange slice and 1 lemon slice with ice cubes in each of 4 tall glasses.

Pour chilled lemonade over the ice and citrus slices. Makes 4 servings.

* *Brands may vary by region; substitute a similar product.*

Sunkist

Strawberry Orange Smoothie
Dannon

1 pint fresh strawberries (or 2 cups frozen strawberries)

1 cup (or two 4-ounce containers) Dannon* Light & Fit 0% Plus strawberry nonfat yogurt

1/2 cup unsweetened orange juice

1 tablespoon chopped fresh mint, plus leaves for garnish

2 teaspoons sugar (optional)

5 ice cubes

Combine strawberries, yogurt, orange juice, chopped mint, sugar and ice cubes in a blender.

Pulse until well combined and ice is crushed.

Serve in tall glasses. Garnish with mint leaves. Makes 2 servings.

Brands may vary by region; substitute a similar product.

Ocean Breeze Cooler
Dole

4 large Dole* bananas, peeled

1 12-ounce can frozen pineapple juice concentrate, thawed, divided

1 pint mango *or* pineapple sorbet, thawed

2 liters diet *or* regular ginger ale

2 cups fresh Dole* Tropical Gold Pineapple, cut into chunks

Dole* red grapes (optional) for garnish

Sliced oranges and sliced limes, for garnish

Combine 2 bananas and half of the thawed juice concentrate in a blender or food processor. Cover and blend until smooth.

In a large punch bowl, stir together banana mixture, sorbet and remaining thawed juice concentrate. Add ginger ale.

Slice remaining bananas; add to the punch with pineapple chunks and fruit garnish. Makes 17 servings.

Brands may vary by region; substitute a similar product.

Cranberry Punch with Orange Sherbet
Kirkland Signature/Cliffstar

6 cups Kirkland Signature Cranberry Juice Cocktail

12 ounces frozen limeade, thawed

3 cups apple juice

3 cups orange juice

1 quart orange sherbet

Orange slices, for garnish

In a large bowl, combine cranberry juice, limeade, apple juice and orange juice. Refrigerate until chilled.

To serve, cut sherbet into chunks and add to the bowl. Garnish with orange slices. Makes 20 servings.

Iced Cappuccino
The Hershey Company

2/3 cup Hershey's Syrup, chilled

2 cups cold coffee

2 cups vanilla ice cream

Ice cubes or crushed ice

Whipped topping (optional)

Ground cinnamon (optional)

Place syrup and coffee in a blender container; cover and blend on high speed.

Add ice cream; cover and blend until smooth.

Serve immediately over ice. Top with whipped topping and ground cinnamon, if desired. Makes 6 servings.

Tip: For a lower-fat version, use reduced-fat vanilla ice cream and fat-free whipped topping.

Coffee Nog
Kirkland Signature

2 glass mugs
4 ounces eggnog
4 ounces strong brewed Kirkland
  Signature premium whole-bean
  coffee, or two 2-ounce
  espresso shots

Sugar (optional)
1 ounce brandy, rum or Irish cream
  (optional)
Whipped cream
Grated nutmeg

Fill the mugs with hot water to warm them.

In a pan, gently heat eggnog, but do not allow to boil. Add coffee and stir.

Pour water out of the mugs. Pour eggnog/coffee mixture into the mugs. Add sugar if desired.

Float liquor on top by pouring it slowly over an inverted spoon into each mug.

Top with whipped cream and a generous sprinkle of nutmeg. Makes 2 servings.

Chocolate Coffee
Kirkland Signature

2 glass mugs

8 ounces strong brewed Kirkland Signature premium whole-bean coffee, or four 2-ounce espresso shots

4 tablespoons grated chocolate from your favorite chocolate bar

2 ounces chocolate liqueur (or chocolate syrup for nonalcoholic version)

Sugar (optional)

2 ounces cream, half-and-half or milk (optional)

Whipped cream

Pour hot water into the mugs to warm them for a few minutes.

Pour water out of the mugs and pour coffee into each mug.

Add 1 tablespoon grated chocolate to each mug and stir.

Add chocolate liqueur or chocolate syrup to each mug and stir.

Add sugar if desired.

Add cream, half-and-half or milk if desired.

Top with whipped cream and sprinkle liberally with remaining chocolate pieces. Makes 2 servings.

Tip: For interesting variations, substitute coffee liqueur or Irish cream for the chocolate liqueur.

Index

A

Ahi
    in Niçoise salad, 26
    seared, appetizer, 50
Apple pear cake, 207
Apples
    cake, German, 210
    crêpes, cherry, 33
    crisp, 115
    crisp, pear, 193
    in fruit salad, 29
    glazed, in caramel sauce, 187
    Gouda ladder loaf, 212
    with ham, cider-glazed, 126
    pancake, German, 34
    pie, cranberry, 202
    pie, Dutch, 202
    salad with creamy provolone dressing, 58
    salad, salmon, 140
    salad, spinach, chicken and, 57
    salsa, 41
    stir-fry, chicken, 14
    in trifle, fruit, 29
Applesauce, in banana-carrot loaf, 34
Apricots
    crisp, peach and amaretti, 192
    martini, 183
Arancini, spinach, 45
Asian pear. See apple pear
Asparagus
    crostini, 49
    grilled, wrapped in prosciutto, 46
    prosciutto rolls, 44
    and salmon stir-fry, 138
    in spring bouquet salad, 58
Avocados
    caprese salad, 67
    chicken salad with, 63
    French bean salad with, 13
    salad, clementine, celery and radish, 70
    salad, grape tomato, 66
    sandwich, ham and spicy mayo, 179
    skewered chicken with, 48

B

Bacon
    chowder, caramelized onion, 72
    and green bean casserole, 81

    slaw, Napa cabbage and carrot, 95
Bagel chips with spinach artichoke cream cheese
    dip, 47
Bananas
    carrot loaf, 34
    Nutella stuffed croissant, 35
    in ocean breeze cooler, 218
    smoothie, strawberry, 217
    in vanilla almond bars coconut pie, 200
Bars
    energy, 39
    lemon gingerbread, 214
    tiramisu cheesecake, 214
Beans, French green
    hazelnut and lemon, 16
    salad with avocado and mango, 13
Beans, green, canned
    casserole, bacon, 81
    in pasta primavera, 171
Beef
    burgers, fajita, 123
    burgers, mini meatloaf, 125
    chuck, pot roast, 119
    ground, in peppered chopped steak, 26
    meatballs, 169
    pot roast, 119
    prime rib roast with fennel, 119
    sirloin patties and portobello stew, 120
    steak au poivre, 89
    steak, flank, citrus-marinated, 121
    steak, flank, sandwich, 124
    steak, Montreal peppered, 120
    steaks, spicy lime, 122
    steaks, strip, pepper-crusted, 113
    tri-tip fajitas, 172
Blackberries
    in breakfast smoothie bowl, 12
    in grape and fruit pizza, 196
    with lemon tarts, 197
    in spinach salad, 15
    in trifle, 183
Blueberries
    in breakfast smoothie bowl, 12
    cobbler, cherry, 192
    dried, in cream cheese puffs, 212
    in grape and fruit pizza, 196
    parfait, cantaloupe, 189
    salad, fennel, 57
    in spinach salad, 15
    in trifle, 183

    in trifle, fruit, 29
Bread
    banana-carrot loaf, 34
    coffee pumpkin, 213
Bread, prepared
    ciabatta roll, in vegetarian sandwich, 178
    ciabatta rolls, in panini, 181
    demi baguette, in antipasto sandwich, 178
    demi baguette, in steak sandwich, 124
    multi-grain, in turkey avocado sprout club
        sandwiches, 16
    whole grain, in ham, spicy mayo and avocado
        sandwich, 179
Breakfast casserole, 36
Breakfast energy bar poppers, 39
Broccoli
    in quiche, 175
    in stir-fry, 19
Broccoli rabe, in stir-fry, 19
Brownie bites, in s'more, 215
Brunch dishes
    breakfast casserole, 36
    egg casserole, 37
    taquito skillet, 39
Bruschetta, chicken and vegetable, 49
Burgers
    beef fajita, 123
    mini meatloaf, 125
Butter
    in bacon and caramelized onion chowder, 72
    in chocolate silk pie, 201
    cranberry orange, 82
    maple, 82
    southwestern, 82

C

Cabbage, bacon and carrot slaw, 95
Cakes
    apple pear, 207
    chocolate, prepared, with berries, 206
    German raw apple, 210
    orange dream chiffon, 206
Calzone, Italian sausage, 165
Cantaloupe
    and blueberry parfaits, 189
    in fruit kebabs with cinnamon cream, 27
    in fruit salad, 29
Cappuccino, iced, 219
Caramels, sea salt, 90

Supplier Listing

ACH Foods, Inc /Mazola Oils, 129
www.mazola.com
1-866-4MAZOLA

Acme Food Sales, 128
www.acmefood.com
206-762-5150

Aconex, 185, 195
www.aconex.cl
011-56-2-9413312

Alaska Glacier Seafoods,132
www.alaskaglacierseafoods.com
907-790-3590

Alpine Fresh, Inc., 12, 16, 22, 25, 46
www.alpinefresh.com
800-292-8777

Alsum Produce, 81
www.alsum.com
800-236-5127

AMC Direct Inc., 160
www.amcdirect.net

American Fish & Seafood Co., 148
www.americanfish.com
213-612-0350

American Pride Seafoods, 145, 156
www.americanprideseafoods.com
508-997-0031

Andrew & Williamson Fresh Produce, 15
www.andrew-williamson.com
619-661-6000

Ann's House of Nuts, 55
800-466-2667

Anthony Farms, 81
www.anthonyfarms.com
800-826-0456

Anthony Vineyards, Inc., 53
www.anthonyvineyards.com
661-858-6211

Apio, Inc., 174, 175
www.apioinc.com
800-454-1355

Apple & Eve, 184
www.appleandeve.com
800-969-8018

Aquagold, 138
954-888-9445

Aquamericas/Fresh Tilapia Fillets, 152
www.aquamericas.com
800-569-8323

Atlantic Capes Fisheries, 144
www.atlanticcapes.com
508-990-9040

Atlantic Veal & Lamb, Inc., 116, 117
800-222-VEAL

Australian Lamb Company, 102, 103, 104
www.auslamb.com

Bard Valley Medjool Date Growers, 68
www.bardmedjool.com
928-726-9191

Barry Callebaut, 199
www.barry-callebaut.com
802-524-9711

BC Hot House Foods, Inc., 172
www.bchothouse.com
800-663-1889

BelGioioso Cheese Inc., 52, 58
www.belgioioso.com
920-863-2123

Best Brands Corp., 68, 82, 83
www.bestbrandscorp.com
800-866-3300

Boskovich Farms, Inc., 56, 57
www.boskovichfarms.com
805-487-2299

Bravante Produce, 148
www.bravanteproduce.com

Cabot Creamery Cooperative, 44
www.cabotcheese.coop
888-792-2268

Calavo Growers, 48, 67
www.calavo.com
805-525-1245

California Avocado Commission, 48, 67
www.californiaavocado.com

California Pear Advisory Board, 187
www.calpear.com
916-441-0432

California Walnut Commission, 21
www.walnuts.org
916-932-7070

Cal Maine Foods, 37
www.calmainefoods.com
601-948-6813

Camanchaca Inc., 134, 135
www.camanchacainc.com
800-335-7553

Campbell's, 49
www.campbellsoup.com
800-257-8443

Cardile Bros. Mushrooms, Inc., 175
www.cardilebrothersmushrooms.com
610-268-2470

Catania Worldwide, 33
www.cataniaworldwide.com
416-236-9394

Cecelia Packing Corporation, 160
www.ceceliapack.com
559-626-5000

Cedar Key Aquaculture Farms, 50
www.cedarkeyclams.com

Chelan Fresh, 193
www.chelanfresh.com
509-682-3854

Cherry Central, 205
www.cherrycentral.com
800-678-1860

Chestnut Hill Farms, 130
www.chfusa.com
305-592-6969

Chicken of the Sea, 180, 181
www.chickenofthesea.com

Chilean Avocado Importers Assoc., 63
www.chileanavocado.org
831-689-0962

Clear Springs Foods, 158
ww.clearsprings.com
800-635-8211

CM Holtzinger Fruit Co., 210
www.holtzingerfruit.com
509-249-4232

Coleman Natural Foods, 20
www.ColemanNatural.com
800-442-8666

Columbia Marketing International, 186, 187
www.cmiapples.com
509-663-1955

Conagra Foods, 173
www.conagrafoods.com
813-241-1500

Cottage Bakery, 178
www.cottagebakery.com
209-365-5459

Countryside Baking, 208
www.dawnfoods.com
800-478-4252

Curry & Company, Inc., 15
www.curryandco.com
503-393-6033

Custom Blending, Inc., 188
www.rodellevanilla.com
970-482-8845

Dakota Beef, LLC., 123
www.dakotaorganic.com
605-772-5669

Daniele International, 181
www.danielefoods.com
800-451-2535